TEACHING CHRISTIAN VALUES IN THE FAMILY

A GUIDE FOR PARENTS

By Jim Larson, Ph.D.

Illustrations by Tony Kenyon

Edited by Dave and Neta Jackson

David C. Cook Publishing Co., 1982 Elgin, Illinois — Weston, Ontario

CONTENTS

TRANSPARENCIES
1. Vital Questions Regarding Values
2. Factors Influencing Moral Development
3. Levels of Moral Development
4. Importance of the Family
5. Social Development
6. Kinds of Values
7. Sources of Guidance for Christians
8. Rotating Discussion Groups
9. Jesus Christ and Our Values
10. Essential Christian Values
11. Christian Values Versus Secular Values
12. Values and the Home Environment
13. Styles of Family Leadership
14. Teaching in the Family
15. Problems, Problems, Problems
16. Celebration Songs

REPRODUCTION MASTERS
1. Course Schedule
2. A Family Story
3. Coat of Arms
4. Developing Values
5. Developing Values (Page 2)
6. Jesus and Values
7. Christian Values
8. Conflicting Values
9. Responsibilities of Parenting
10. Communication in the Family
11. Family Activities That Build Values
12. Guidelines for Working Through Differences
13. Case Studies
14. Looking Back, Looking Forward
15. Evaluation of Learning Experience
16. Celebration Responsive Reading

PERSONALLY SPEAKING

Families today are plagued by pressures and changes which threaten to pull many of them apart. With increased mobility, a materialistic society, role changes, the knowledge explosion, problems of urban living, and many more perplexities, conflicting systems of values seem to come at us from every direction.

According to Carl Rogers,

The modern individual is assailed from every angle by divergent and contradictory value claims. It is no longer possible, as it was in the not too distant historical past, to settle comfortably into the value system of one's forebears or one's community and live out one's life without ever examining the nature and the assumptions of that system . . . . Value orientations from the past appear to be in a state of disintegration or collapse.[1]

When confronted by these realities, people may find themselves feeling both perplexed and frustrated—perplexed as to what is really right or wrong any-more; frustrated with the complexity of many issues they face today.

Family research consistently reports that the moral development of children is most strongly affected by the family relationships, despite the multitude of other influences which affect our children.

Christian parents are called by God to train children in the way they should go. The Church has the opportunity today to enhance the leadership potential parents have for guiding the development of positive Christian values in the family.

The purpose of this course is to provide people with a forum for dealing with this vital question of values, helping parents to deal with questions such as:

· What should be our response to the changing values we face?

· What can we do to facilitate the development of values which are both Christ-centered and relevant to today's world?

· How are values taught?

My hope and prayer is that God will continue to guide us, as members of the Body of Christ, to seek innovative and constructive ways to support and nurture parents, so that they in turn may become the kind of mature leaders and effective examples that God has called them to be.

My prayers are with you as you prepare to teach this course.

Cordially,

Jim Larson

Jim Larson

Note
[1]Carl Rogers, "Toward a Modern Approach to Values: The Valuing Process in the Mature Person," in *Readings in Values Clarification* (Minneapolis: Winston Press, 1973), p. 75.

Goals for the Course

As you begin to make plans for teaching a course to parents on developing values in the family, you need to identify the major goals for the course. All the session objectives and other concerns can be understood within the context of the following course goals:

Identify Scriptural Guidelines for Dealing with Moral Concerns

In a world where there are many conflicting values, we need to acknowledge the authority we have as followers of Jesus Christ to make moral decisions, because of the revelation provided in God's Word.

As we identify Scriptural guidelines for dealing with moral concerns, we will be confronted with questions such as the following:
· What is our guide as Christians regarding values?
· How do we interpret Scriptures regarding ethical and moral concerns?
· What role does the church play?
· How important are reason and conscience?
· How does the Holy Spirit help us make personal decisions?
· Specifically, what are the teachings of Jesus which should most significantly influence our values?
· What do we learn from the example of Jesus regarding values?

Describe Important Christian Values

There is significant difference of opinion among some Christians as to what are Christian values. Parents can profit from dealing with concerns such as the following:
· How are Christian values different from secular values?
· What do we do when our values conflict?
· What values are left to the individual discretion of each person?

Describe How Moral Development Takes Place

The process of developing values begins at birth and continues throughout the life cycle. Just how this process takes place will be essential to know as we seek to develop values in our families.

Questions such as these will be critical for our consideration:
· What are the different stages of moral development, beginning with young children and continuing through adolescence into adulthood?
· What causes some people to stop growing in their moral development?
· How do other developmental concerns (such as self-esteem and social development) for children and adolescents influence the development of values?
· How do parents' values influence the values of children?

Plan Specific Ways in the Family to Help Children Develop Christian Values

Values do not develop in a vacuum; they are formed in a family environment which may be healthy or unhealthy. The quality of that environment greatly influences the kinds of values children adopt.

Among the concerns related to this objective are the following:
· How can parents strengthen loving relationships with their children?
· How can the home environment be both just and intellectually stimulating?
· How much freedom is appropriate for children and adolescents as they learn to make their own decisions?
· What should parents do when they feel their children are making wrong decisions?

Acknowledge and Strengthen One's Role As a Model for Christian Attitudes and Behaviors

Research consistently shows that the most potent influence parents can have on their children's moral development is by the example they set. Actions and attitudes seem to speak louder and more indelibly than words.

Parents will deal with concerns such as these:
· What does it mean to be a "model" when it comes to moral development?
· How can parents evaluate the kind of examples they have been?
· How can parents strengthen the examples they set for their children?
· How are parents influenced by their children?

Develop a Support System with Other Parents

Many parents report feelings of alienation or loneliness when dealing with parent-child conflicts. Parents may feel they are the only persons experiencing particular difficulties. This seems to be especially true for parents of adolescents.

Through sharing mutual concerns and praying for each other, parents will be able to help shoulder each other's burdens, as concerns such as these are considered:

· What are typical conflicts which families face regarding values?

· What are various ways other parents have responded and dealt with conflicts and difficulties at home?

· How can sharing these concerns with other parents help reduce the stress and strengthen relationships in the family?

· What are specific ways we can encourage and support other families?

Keep these overall objectives in mind as you prepare to teach this class.

Planning Your Schedule

TEACHING CHRISTIAN VALUES IN THE FAMILY is a 13-session course for parents and other interested adults. All 13 sessions are designed to include the following components and dynamics.

Getting Started (10-15 minutes)

Each session should begin with a welcome and an opening prayer asking God to guide the group as they deal with complex issues.

Getting Started provides the group with a theme-related activity which will guide parents to:

· Get acquainted with other parents;
· Build a sense of togetherness;
· Get oriented to each theme in an informal way.

Most of the activities in the Getting Started time will be done in small groups, although on occasion there may be large-group involvement as well.

Exploring Together (15-20 minutes)

Exploring Together involves the presentation of basic information related to each session theme in a large-group setting.

Despite the fact that the Exploring Together time is primarily lecture-oriented, the teacher will find that keeping the presentation rather informal and encouraging dialogue will enhance the learning process. *Information that you can read directly to the group, or that you might want to rephrase in your own words are printed in italic type, like this sentence.*

In addition to the presentation material for each session, reproduction masters and transparencies are provided to maximize the effectiveness of the teacher. Be sure that an adequate number of copies of the necessary reproduction masters have been made before each session.

Sharing Together (20-25 minutes)

Sharing Together, usually done in small groups of two to six people, provides the setting for participants to interact on questions related to the session theme, as well as to share insights, encouragements, and concerns.

Most people are comfortable sharing in a smaller group; therefore, a variety of small-group activities will enhance the learning experience for everyone.

Family Application (5-10 minutes)

After people have been involved in small groups, they will be reconvened in the large group to consider the application of one Biblical value as an example. Using the insights of the session, parents will have a chance to think through how they might specifically work on that value in their families. At the end of the course they will have been guided through 13 Biblical examples, and in so doing, they will have gained the skills for developing other Christian values in their homes.

Wrap-Up (5 minutes)

During Wrap-Up, the leader briefly summarizes the issues and concerns of the session. In this way, the essential thoughts which have been learned are presented one last time in capsule form to reinforce the learning that has already taken place.

Schedule Options

The basic design for this course is a 60-minute *Sunday school class* for adults. Ample resources are provided for this option, whether the class is an age-level class, or a special elective.

If only 30 to 40 minutes are available, most of the activities, as well as the input time, can be reduced proportionately to fit within a shortened time schedule.

The same basic options as those described for the Sunday morning class can be used in *weekday study groups*. In a small-group, home setting, leadership can be shared by group members. If desired, input can be condensed and more time provided for the various discussion activities.

This course can also be adapted to two *weekend workshops or retreats*. Consider offering this course as a community outreach on Friday evening and Saturday for two weekends.

Equipment and Supplies

You should have access to these items in teaching this course:

· Overhead projector and screen
· Chalkboard
· Chalk, pencils, felt pens
· Writing and drawing paper, index cards (3 x 5-inch)
· Masking tape, scissors, glue
· Newsprint tablet or roll of butcher paper

UNIT 1 · VALUES AND THE FAMILY CONNECTION

Focus

God has provided the family as an important means of developing values.

Scripture Background

Genesis 2:18; Deuteronomy 4:9, 10; 6:6-9; Psalm 139:15; Matthew 7:11, 20; II Corinthians 12:14; Ephesians 6:1.

Unit Objectives—*To help people:*

· GET ACQUAINTED with other people in the group.
· DESCRIBE how values develop.
· IDENTIFY specific ways the family influences moral development.
· REFINE and EVALUATE their own personal values.

For Your Reflection . . .

The word *family* may bring a flood of different thoughts, recollections, and feelings to your mind. What does the word *family* mean to you? Reflect upon your own family background. How did your parents affect your values?

God designed families in which to grow up, experience loving relationships, learn values, and see firsthand how those values work.

In this first unit of study, you will have opportunity to guide people as they reflect upon the importance of the family in developing values.

What can you do to provide a learning environment which is safe, comfortable, and caring?

Take a few moments to thank God for this chance to teach these truths regarding Christian values. Ask for wisdom to teach clearly and flexibly in a way which meets the needs of your group.

UNIT HIGHLIGHTS

Session	Getting Started (10-15 minutes)	Exploring Together (15-20 minutes)	Sharing Together (20-25 minutes)	Family Application (5-10 minutes) Teaching the Value of . . .
1	Get-Acquainted Interviews	Introduction and Definitions TR-1; RM-1	Brainstorming	Friendship
2	Values Continuum	Stages of Moral Development TR-2, 3	Small Group Discussions	Justice, Mercy, and Humility
3	Structured Sharing	The Importance of the Family TR-4, 5	Values Refinement RM-2	A Good Spouse
4	Name Tag Activity RM-3	Identifying Personal Values TR-6; RM-4, 5	Covenant Groups	Generosity

UNIT 1 · VALUES AND THE FAMILY CONNECTION
SESSION 1 · INTRODUCTORY SESSION

Objectives—To help people:

· GET ACQUAINTED with other participants in the group.
· DEFINE the word *value*.
· IDENTIFY several struggles or conflicts regarding values which people experience today.

Advance Preparation

Have available:
1. TR-1 ("Vital Questions Regarding Values").
2. An overhead projector and a screen.
3. Copies of RM-1 ("Course Schedule") in sufficient quantity for your group. (Be sure you have the appropriate information for class members to fill in the blanks after you pass out the sheets.)
4. A chalkboard or newsprint tablet.
5. Blank paper and pencils for the group discussions.

Getting Started: Get-Acquainted Interviews (10-15 minutes)

Welcome everyone to your group. Begin this session with prayer, asking God to guide people as they deal with these vital issues related to values and our families.

Ask the people to get together in groups of two, preferably with someone they do not know very well. Encourage the people to get acquainted by interviewing each other. In addition to basic information regarding the other individual and his or her family, partners should find out why each person is interested in taking this course. What are one or two questions each person would like to deal with in this course?

If your group numbers less than 12-15, ask each person to introduce his or her partner to the entire group by sharing what each learned about that person.

If your group numbers more than 12-15, have partners introduce each other in groups of 8-12 people.

As people share, create a composite list of concerns and questions on chalkboard or newsprint.

If you have had to break your total group up into groups of 8-12, assign a recorder for each of those groups, and then create a composite list from the contributions of each subgroup.

If you are not bound by time, it might be nice to have coffee and tea available for people to enjoy during this time.

Exploring Together: Introduction and Definitions (15-20 minutes)

1. Introduction

This course will help us appreciate the importance of the family, especially as it relates to the development of values.

We live in a world which is marked by rapid changes and uncertainties. For example:

· *Approximately three-fourths of the knowledge now available to human beings has been learned since the end of World War II. Futurists (researchers who study the future) estimate that society will increase its fund of knowledge by more than six times in the next 35 years.*

· *The technological revolution has intensified the feelings of alienation and meaninglessness which many people find in their jobs, relationships, and everyday life.*

· *Relationships between men and women, and between parents and children, have also been experiencing significant changes and strains.*

What are some feelings people may have as they encounter all of these changes? (Allow a moment or two for people to mention their ideas: fear, frustration, longings for simpler times, hope, and so on.)

It is especially important in times like these that we identify and live according to a system of Christian values. Our values can provide an anchor for us, a solid foundation for handling the perplexities and challenges we encounter.

There are other value systems, such as materialism, by which many people live. Our purpose here is to identify the kind of Christian values which can honor God, help us cope with life, and strengthen family relationships.

For these reasons, we will be dealing with a number of vital questions regarding values and our families. (Display TR-1, "Vital Questions Regarding Values," and briefly go over the questions listed on the transparency.)

Distribute copies of the "Course Schedule" (RM-1), which describes in greater detail the format and content for this course. Have the participants fill in the dates and other information, and then take a moment or two to answer any questions. Be sure participants understand that in addition to lecture, there will be group discussions and other activities to strengthen the learning experience and make it practical.

2. Definition and Framework

Mention that as you start this study of values and the family, you need to define terms and build

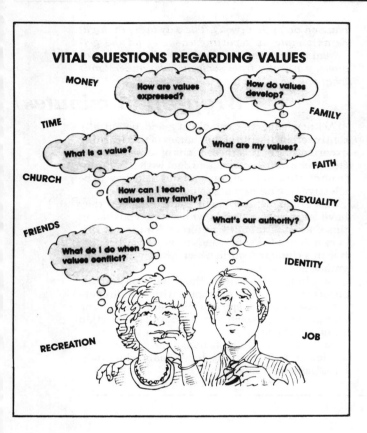

VITAL QUESTIONS REGARDING VALUES

MONEY

How are values expressed?

How do values develop?

FAMILY

TIME

What is a value?

What are my values?

FAITH

CHURCH

How can I teach values in my family?

SEXUALITY

What's our authority?

FRIENDS

What do I do when values conflict?

IDENTITY

RECREATION

JOB

values is a lifelong process. As a person develops, values also change and develop. What someone values one year may or may not be what is important to him or her in the future. For instance, the value of work is learned. And as most of you parents know, it takes some years of experience before youngsters can agree with Proverbs 14:23: "All hard work brings a profit, but mere talk leads only to poverty."

What are examples of some of the other values which can change over a period of time? (Allow a few moments for people to name their ideas, as you write them down on chalkboard or newsprint. Since this is a brainstorming exercise, do not discuss or evaluate the ideas suggested. Examples: clothing styles, music, leisure activities, involvements in church and community, etc.)

If there is any group which has the resources and authority to deal with these changing values and all of the changes which affect our families, it is the Church. Our faith in Jesus Christ provides us with an authority and perspective for identifying what our values should be and how we can live according to Christian values.

And despite the great multitude of influences which affect our children and young people, we as parents can have significant impact upon the moral development of each member of our families. The Scriptures tell us this (Deut. 11:18-21); so do a great number of family researchers today.

Sharing Together: Brainstorming (20-25 minutes)

Mention that there are a great number of struggles people experience today which involve feelings, preferences, and values.

Divide the group into smaller groups of three or four. Ask each group to brainstorm (list without discussion or evaluation) ideas as to what some of these typical value conflicts might be. If the group seems unsure of the assignment, think together of an example or two to get started. (For example, conflict over the use of time—job versus family; uses of money, etc.)

Tell groups that they will have approximately eight to ten minutes to make their lists. Ask groups to appoint recorders to write down their ideas.

After about ten minutes, reassemble in a larger group. Ask the recorders of the groups to read their lists as you make a composite on the chalkboard or newsprint.

Underline which conflicts group members agree

a foundation regarding the study.

What is a value? Webster's New Collegiate Dictionary *defines a value as "relative worth, utility, or importance; degree of excellence; something intrinsically valuable or desirable." A Scriptural example of this can be found in Ecclesiastes 7:1: "A good name is better than fine perfume." This is a declaration of relative worth.*

A moral is a principle of right or wrong. So, moral development is the development of feelings and attitudes about what is right or wrong. And it is often our values—what we consider to be of great importance—which influence our feelings regarding rightness or wrongness for us in any situation. In this context the verse, "Faith by itself, if it is not accompanied by action, is dead" (Jas. 2:17), is a value or statement of relative worth and becomes the foundation for a moral principle.

People are valuing creatures. They prefer some things over others in terms of usefulness or general worth. People do not only know and feel—they can also value.

Values are not established permanently early in life, never to be modified or changed. Developing

are most common. Then ask the group which conflicts they feel are most damaging to family relationships today. Place an asterisk (*) next to each of those items.

Family Application (5-10 minutes)

Teaching the value of friendship.

At the beginning of class we spent time getting to know one another. For some children and young people that process involves feelings ranging from mild anxiety to paralyzing fear, and yet there is a real value in friendship. Proverbs 18:24 says, "A man that hath friends must shew himself friendly" (KJV).

Why select such a simple value as a first example? For two reasons: Don't begin with the most hotly contested issues. But do begin with something where you can have some empathy for the struggles your children face. If you can't remember how hard it was for you to stick to the job when you were first learning to do the dishes, then don't begin by trying to preach about the value of work. Instead, begin by sharing yourself—maybe the discomfort you feel in trying to meet new people, but the importance you

place on doing it anyway. The way to begin might be as simple as reporting casually on the get-acquainted part of this session. Values are contagious, especially from someone who understands what you face.

Wrap-Up (5 minutes)

Acknowledge the complexity and potentially controversial nature of the themes of this learning experience. Yet it is these kinds of difficult issues God wants us to confront and deal with as we grow in our faith and in our understanding of how to be effective, loving parents to our children.

Ask group members to list something new they have learned or concerns which were clarified in this session. (Examples: different families experience many of the same kinds of value conflicts; we live in a changing world which greatly affects our values and morals; etc.)

Conclude with prayer, thanking God for this opportunity to learn, to grapple with complex subjects. Ask God for a spirit of openness as the group learns together about how to develop Christian values in the family.

Be sure to be available at the conclusion of the session to talk with any individuals who might have personal concerns.

SESSION 2 · HOW DO VALUES DEVELOP?

Objectives—To help people:

· CLARIFY initial feelings regarding how values develop.
· IDENTIFY factors which influence moral development.
· DESCRIBE the various levels of moral development.
· IDENTIFY typical moral conflicts or concerns for each age level.

Advance Preparation

Have available:
1. TR-2 ("Factors Influencing Moral Development") and TR-3 ("Levels of Moral Development").
2. An overhead projector and screen.
3. A chalkboard or newsprint.
4. Several sheets of blank paper and pencils for group discussions.

Getting Started: Values Continuum (10-15 minutes)

Welcome everyone to this second session. Again, begin with prayer, asking God to guide the participants as they seek to deepen their understanding of how values develop.

Tell participants that this session's opening activity will help them clarify or identify some of their opinions and feelings regarding how values develop.

Designate a line across your room—an area cleared of chairs. This will be a continuum, or line, upon which people will stand to express their opinions. Identify one end of the line as "Strongly Agree," the other end "Strongly Disagree." The midpoint of the line will be for opinions which are neutral or ambivalent.

Tell people that as each statement is read, they are to move to a place on the line which designates their opinions and feelings. Once people have moved, briefly discuss each statement together.

Statements to use for the activity:

1. People's values usually don't change.
2. Children usually have the same values as their parents.
3. Adolescents usually have the same values as their parents.
4. Adolescents are influenced more by their friends than by their parents.
5. People's actions always match their values.
6. Values are influenced more by feelings than beliefs.
7. The ability of persons to think has a lot to do with their values.

Exploring Together: Stages of Moral Development (15-20 minutes)

1. Introduction

Briefly review some of the key concepts from the previous session. Emphasize that values develop and change as people grow up.

Values do not develop in a vacuum in which they are unaffected by other areas of development. Moral development is part of the overall process of growth which every person experiences.

We are reminded by the psalmist of the wonders of our creation when he said: "I will praise thee; for I am fearfully and wonderfully made" (Ps. 139:14, KJV).

Every person is unique. Scientists tell us that children of the same parents may have any of 280 billion different chromosome combinations! Thus, even children within the same family can be quite different in their looks, temperaments, and feelings, even though they are exposed to similar influences and experiences.

An interesting feature of human nature is that each person possesses an inner clock which determines his or her own rate of development. Even though most people will go through similar stages of growth from infancy to being fully mature, the rate of development can vary widely from person to person.

2. Influencing Factors

There are a number of important factors which influence the kinds of values a person develops, especially during the childhood and adolescent years. (Refer to TR-2, "Factors Influencing Moral Development.")

a. Self-Esteem

Self-concept is the image that a person has of himself. It is an awareness of being separate from one's surroundings. And this self-concept has certain feelings attached to it—whether the person feels lovable, worthy, and competent, or unlovable, worthless, and incapable. These feelings related to self-concept determine the level of self-esteem a person has.

Self-esteem is influenced by a number of factors, including the parents' expectations, the physical well-being of the child, the rate of biological maturation, school demands, attitudes of other family members, the dynamics within each family, the opinions of friends and neighbors, and so on.

Healthy self-esteem is quite different from conceit. Conceit is a feeling of superiority towards others and is often based upon deep-seated feelings of inferiority. Healthy self-esteem, on the other hand, is a realistic assessment of one's strengths and weaknesses, a feeling of being equal with others.

Self-esteem is important for a number of reasons:

A person's behavior becomes consistent with one's concept of self.

People who see themselves as inferior will usually act this way, and thus seem inferior to others. The process becomes a vicious cycle in which feelings of inferiority actually lead to inferiority. Such feelings of inadequacy or failure can affect school achievement and relationships with others, as well as values.

On the other hand, children who see themselves as lovable and adequate will tend to be more confident and willing to try new tasks. Such children will be able to stand up for what they believe, whether or not their peers agree with their values.

Persons with adequate self-esteem usually are better able to cope with the stresses of life.

Stress is inevitable in life. Persons with poor self-esteem often spend a great deal of time denying or distorting their feelings and opinions. This creates anxiety and is a source of tension. Often such people feel threatened and become reactors rather than initiators in life, feeling more like victims or martyrs than people with control and responsibility in life.

Persons with healthy self-esteem, on the other hand, are usually more realistic, accepting, in touch with feelings, able to cope, and have happier relationships with other people.

b. Social Development

Being able to relate to others and form satisfying relationships—through the process we call social development—is a very important part of growing up. And learning to be social is a lifelong process which begins at birth.

Children's first and most formative social learning takes place in the family. In earliest childhood, children tend to play independently of each other and watch each other. They often have difficulty playing together. Through increasing contacts with others, children are able to handle group experiences for longer periods of time.

As children mature, there is a growing development of empathy and sympathy towards others, with greater capability to share and be concerned about the needs of others. Most children and young people learn with increasing ease how to have friends and be friends to others.

Social development influences values in a number of ways. For example, people who have an extremely high need to please others or to be included by others will often be willing to bend or change values in order to have that need met.

c. Intellectual Development

Intellectual development is the growth of the ability to reason. It is learning to know, in contrast to learning to feel or to do. Intellectual growth is influenced by such factors as the maturation of the nervous system, interaction with one's surroundings, social pressures, and the general tendency to seek organization and structure.

Researchers have found that even though the rate of development will vary widely from child to child, the sequence in the growth of the ability to reason is quite similar for everyone. Researcher Jean Piaget (pronounced Zhahn Pee-ah-ZHAY) has discovered that there are several stages children experience as they grow intellectually:[1]

Sensorimotor or Action Intelligence Stage (birth to 2 years).

Piaget maintains that infants are learning to coordinate their nerves, senses, and muscles which produce behavior, and that knowledge develops through interaction with people and objects. For the very dependent newborn, such learning is simple but critical for later learning. Children in the Sensorimotor Stage live in the present and cannot understand how to wait for something in the future.

Preoperational or Prelogical Stage (approximately ages 2 to 7).

Children in this stage are energetically involved in acquiring language, the ability to communicate through words with other people. Children still are thinking at this stage in rather simple ways. They are literal and factual but still cannot be logical.

Concrete Operations Stage (approximately ages 7 to 11).

Children at this level have increased ability to use reasoning power and symbolic thinking. They are learning to use a variety of ways to solve problems and can compare, contrast, and see similarities and differences.

Formal Operations or Abstract Thinking (approximately age 11 through adult).

As people achieve this stage, they are able to think more abstractly and logically. There are often moral questions regarding fairness, rightness, and wrongness. People at the Formal Operations Stage can deal with difficult questions such as: "What is the purpose of life?" "Who is God?" and "How do I know right from wrong?"

Intellectual development and moral development are not the same process. But these two processes tend to develop along parallel lines. As persons learn to think more logically and abstractly, there is greater ability to deal with moral issues. In this way, intellectual and moral development are quite intertwined.

3. How Moral Development Takes Place

Researcher Lawrence Kohlberg of Harvard University has found that people develop through a series of moral stages as they seek to find balance and meaning in their lives.[2] Kohlberg's research shows that children grow from making moral judgments in terms of immediate, external, physical consequences to judging in terms of internal purposes, norms, and values. According to Kohlberg, becoming moral means to be directed more by internal attitudes and values than by external laws or expectations.

There are three separate levels through which people grow as they learn to think and live morally (Refer to TR-3, "Levels of Moral Development."):

Level I—Preconventional Level.

At this initial level, children are primarily concerned about external happenings, especially receiving rewards and avoiding punishment. What is right or wrong is determined by what is rewarded or punished.

For example, Bobby knows that taking a cookie from the jar without asking permission from a parent is wrong. If Bobby gets caught and punished for disobeying, taking a cookie is seen (at Level I) as wrong; if Bobby does not get caught, then taking a cookie is seen as right.

Greatest concern is felt for one's own personal needs. There is much egocentricity in this earliest moral level.

Level II—Conventional Level

People living at the conventional level try to live up to the expectations of family, group, or nation. There is strong motivation of family, group, or nation. There is strong motivation to conform to what is expected, to perform what is thought to be good or right roles. Good or right behavior is seen at first as what pleases others. Later in this level, the orientation is towards authority and doing one's duties. If a rule says something is right or wrong, then it is right or wrong. Such rules are not be be questioned or challenged.

Level III—Principled Level

Persons who develop to the principled level believe that moral values become defined by shared standards, rights, and duties, not just by conformity to a standard which someone else imposes. There is a desire to consider the needs of the larger society. The most important principle, according to Kohlberg, is that of justice, which involves respect for persons, and a feeling of equality in every relationship.

Whether or not we agree completely with Kohlberg, he does provide a helpful structure for seeing how values develop: from a concern for avoiding punishment and being rewarded, to meeting one's own needs exclusively, to doing only what will be pleasing to others, to conforming to fixed rules and doing one's duty, to making justice and equality most important in every moral judgment.

Kohlberg reminds us that many persons do not move through every level. In fact, many people remain at the first or second levels their entire lives. Kohlberg observes, for example, that most people convicted of crimes and living in prisons have never moved beyond the first level.

However, researchers have discovered that people do have potential for moving to a higher level. There is always the potential for greater understanding of others' points of view and to move beyond what is important only to ourselves.

4. Values: Words or Actions?

What expresses our values—our words, or our actions?

There are many people who may say they have certain values and openly profess them. But people do not always act upon these verbalized values. For example, persons may say that family is most important, but in terms of time and emotional investment, family may be far less important than job or hobbies. So, persons may state a preference or belief, but it may not always be evident in their behavior.

Behaviorally expressed values, on the other hand, go a step further than spoken values, since action is involved. For example, persons who say that family is most important and who then work diligently to structure quality time for family and evaluate job and other outside involvements in terms of their impact on family are showing that family is indeed important.

Thus, when we consider moral development, we need to rely upon more than words. How a person behaves seems to show what is of greatest importance. So, it is those persons whose words and actions express the same values who are morally consistent.

Scriptures certainly teach the importance of our actions. Jesus said, "By their fruit you will recognize them" (Mt. 7:20). And James stated in a similar vein, "As the body without the spirit is dead, so faith without deeds is dead" (Jas. 2:26).

5. Conclusion

To sum up what you have been learning:

· Every person is unique and is created in God's image.

· There are a number of factors which influence moral development, including self-esteem, social development, and intellectual development. Values *do not develop in a vacuum.*

· There are three distinct levels through which people develop morally: from being concerned only about their own needs, to conforming to the expectations of others, to living according to principles of justice and equality. Thus, at each level, values take on new perspectives.

· Our values are expressed most clearly in our actions, rather than our words.

Sharing Together: Small Group Discussion (20-25 minutes)

Mention that there are specific moral concerns and conflicts which are typical to each age level, including preschool-age children, elementary-age children, adolescents, young adults, middle-age adults, and older adults.

Divide the class into small groups, with one age level assigned to each group. If your large group numbers about 12, have pairs of people work together; if your group includes more than 12 people, increase the size of the small groups accordingly.

Ask the groups to list typical moral conflicts and issues (those related to values) for each age level. Give each group a large sheet of newsprint and a felt pen for listing ideas.

After all of the groups have had at least ten minutes to list ideas, reassemble the large group. Ask a representative of each group to share the group's thoughts. As time permits, have the large group identify other value conflicts for each age level.

Family Application (5-10 minutes)

Teaching the value of justice, mercy, and humility.

Redisplay TR-3, "Levels of Moral Development," and then ask the class to turn to Micah 6:8 as you read the value of justice, mercy, and humility expressed there: "He has showed you, O man, what is good. And what does the Lord require of you? To act justly and to love mercy and to walk humbly with your God."

Ask the class to identify how these values might be expressed (if at all) at each of the levels of moral development. If they are expressed, what would be the motivation? What would compel a child at each of the levels of development to express the values of Micah 6:8? What might cause the child to do otherwise?

Apart from external behavior, at what stage has the value become the child's own standard for living? Is there any way a parent can know when that has happened?

God has revealed the importance of these values to us through His Word, but they would mean very little if He did not express them in His actions toward us. In fact, our primary understanding of justice and mercy come by way of God's example. The example of parents toward their children are equally important in communicating values.

Wrap-Up (5 minutes)

Briefly summarize the content of this session. Ask a group member to conclude with prayer, thanking God for the learning which took place.

Notes

[1]Jean Piaget, *The Origin of Intelligence in Children,* second ed. (New York: International Universities Press, 1952).

[2]Lawrence Kohlberg, "The Cognitive-Developmental Approach to Moral Education," *Phi Delta Kappan* (June 1972), 670-677; "Education, Moral Education, and Faith," *Journal of Moral Education* 4, No. 1 (1974), 5-16; "Moral Education for a Society in Moral Transition," *Educational Leadership* (October 1975), 46-54.

SESSION 3 · WHAT IS THE ROLE OF THE FAMILY?

Objectives—To help people:

· SHARE influences of families they grew up in on the development of personal values.
· LIST ways the family is important for moral and spiritual development.
· CLARIFY values regarding family-related issues.

Advance Preparation

Have available:
1. TR-4 ("Importance of the Family") and TR-5 ("Social Development").
2. An overhead projector and screen.
3. Copies of RM-2 ("A Family Story"), one copy per four people. Cut apart the character descriptions ahead of time (one set per group).
4. A chalkboard or newprint.

Getting Started: Structured Sharing (15 minutes)

Welcome everyone to this session, and begin with prayer. Then divide the class into groups of three. Ask people in each small group to identify themselves as person A, B, or C. Person A will have three minutes to share with the other two persons his or her response to this question: How has your family (parents, brothers and sisters, etc.) influenced your development of values?

At the end of three minutes, persons B and C will have one minute to ask questions of clarification. Then the process repeats with person B having three minutes to share and persons A and C having one minute to ask questions, and so on, until all three persons have had opportunity to share.

Be sure that you or someone else keeps careful track of time for this activity.

Exploring Together: The Importance of the Family (15-20 minutes)

1. Changes in Family Life

Ask the group to mention a number of major changes in recent years affecting family life in our society. List ideas on chalkboard or newsprint as the group responds.

Here is some statistical information regarding families and how they are changing:

· In the past 100 years, there has been a 16-fold increase in the divorce rate. Divorces today occur at nearly three times the rate of 1950. Today, one of every three marriages ends in divorce.
· Eighty percent of divorced people eventually remarry.
· It is estimated that four out of every ten children born in the 1970's will spend part of their childhood in a single-parent family, usually with the mother as the head of the household.
· Because people are living longer, marriages that last are lasting longer—47 instead of 34 years. These couples will spend nearly half their married lives alone together without children at home.
· An increasing number of mothers are returning to work outside the home. Today, at least 54 percent of mothers with school-age children and 37 percent of those with preschool-age children are working outside the home.

As a group, briefly discuss how these changes are affecting families today.

2. Importance of the Family

Even though families may be changing, they continue to have great influence on all of their members, from children through adults.

Family researchers generally agree that the family is here to stay and that there are still many ways in which it is essential for healthy development. This opinion is in agreement with Biblical teachings regarding the importance of the family. Let's look at several ways in which the family is very important. (Use TR-4 "Importance of the Family," to illustrate this section.)

SELF-ESTEEM

We saw in our last session that healthy self-esteem has great impact on our behaviors, attitudes, and values. And the early years of childhood—years when family influence is at its greatest—are the most formative for the development of self-esteem.

Children need to feel loved by their parents so that they can perceive themselves as worthy of love. Through giving children a sense of belonging and of being worthwhile and capable, parents encourage them to develop confidence and self-respect in dealing with the changes and stresses of life.

SOCIAL DEVELOPMENT

God created every person with a need for relationships with other people. At the very beginning of Biblical history, God says, "It is not good for the man to be alone" (Gen. 2:18).

The family plays a key role in helping children become social persons. The child's first and most formative social learning takes place in the family. These early experiences are very important in determining the child's attitude towards and expectations of others.

Over the childhood years, there is a growing network of relationships which extends out from parents to other family members and finally to peers and other people. (Use TR-5, Part A, "Relating to Family and Others," to illustrate this point.)

It is true that the family generally provides the first relationships a child will have. And yet, in one sense, the family needs to work itself "out of a job." In other words, one of the main functions of the family is to guide the young child to become more self-reliant, to move beyond the absolute dependence of infancy to the independence of adulthood. Thus, it is through maturing from dependence *to* independence *that persons are best able to become* interdependence—*the healthy combination of self-reliance with mature, loving relationships with other people.* (Use TR-5, Part B, "Growing Toward Interdependence," to illustrate this point.)

"Letting go" of children—encouraging them to become less dependent and more sociable and self-reliant—is one of the most difficult, yet important, tasks of parents.

MORAL DEVELOPMENT

(Return to TR-4, "Importance of the Family.) *For centuries, the family has been acknowledged as having almost an exclusive responsibility for the development of values for its members. And despite the fact that there is an increasing number of influences on the moral development of children, researchers have found that the family continues to be the most significant factor in the healthy development of values.*

The home environment influences everything from personal tastes and preferences, to attitudes regarding other people and values regarding all areas of life.

Young children usually see parents as powerful people, as those who provide love, security, and direction. Children will often imitate the behaviors and attitudes of their parents, since home is the place where they observe values in action in the earliest days of life. (The subject of parents being examples will be discussed in an entire session later in this course.)

Thus, parents influence their children both by what they say (or do not say), as well as by what they do (or do not do). Because children are such perceptive observers, parental example is a more potent influence than words can ever be.

SPIRITUAL DEVELOPMENT

God has created people with a need to be related to Him. This "God-shaped vacuum" can be filled only by God Himself through a growing, dynamic relationship. From the very beginning of Biblical history, the family has been seen as the place where

the legacy of faith can be shared and reproduced. In Deuteronomy 4:9, 10, we read the following:

Only be careful, and watch yourselves closely so that you do not forget the things your eyes have seen or let them slip from your heart as long as you live. Teach them to your children and to their children after them. Remember the day you stood before the Lord your God at Horeb, when he said to me, "Assemble the people before me to hear my words so that they may learn to revere me as long as they live in the land and may teach them to their children.

The Scriptures tell us that teaching and learning about spiritual matters is to take place at home in both formal and informal ways:

These commandments that I give you today are to be upon your hearts. Impress them on your children. Talk about them when you sit at home and when you walk along the road, when you lie down and when you get up. Tie them as symbols on your hands and bind them on your foreheads. Write them on the doorframes of your houses and on your gates (Deut. 6:6-9).

Throughout Scriptures, the role of parent is upheld as vital, even awesome, as providing both joy and grief (see Prov. 10:1). Jesus acknowledged the care of children as a primary human duty and expected parents to be sensitive to the needs of their children (see Mt. 7:11; II Cor. 12:14, and Eph. 6:4).

So, the Christian family is the place where Christian values can be developed and lived out. It is the place where Christlike love and acceptance can be experienced and healthy feelings developed toward God, the Scriptures, the Church, and spiritual matters.

3. Conclusion

We have seen that the family has great influence upon all areas of our development as human beings, including the moral and spiritual areas. The task of being leaders in our families is an awesome task, but one in which God has promised to be with us and to help us develop the wisdom to be the kind of parents He wants us to be.

Sharing Together: Clarifying Values Roleplay (20-25 minutes)

Read the following family situation. Explain to the class that they will be dividing into small groups to roleplay the situation and then evaluate their interaction as "family members."

A FAMILY STORY

Ten-year-old Ben, *while home alone after school, receives a call from the police that his sister* Patty, *age 14, has been picked up for shoplifting. He calls his mother at the clothing shop where she works part-time, who in turn calls her husband through his rug-cleaning business.* Janet *and* Steve, *the parents, go to the police station and pick up Patty, who has been released to their custody, since it is her first offense. The roleplay begins as the family interacts and tries to come to some understanding/ solution/resolution of the situation.*

Now divide the class into small groups of four persons. (If your class is not divisible by four, a few groups can have five, with the fifth person acting as observer and facilitator for the evaluation questions.) Pass out one copy of RM-2 ("A Family Story") to each small group, having first cut apart the character descriptions. Instruct the small groups to assign a character part to each person in the group. Each person should study his or her character silently for a minute, not revealing to the other "family members" the contents of the assigned character slip.

Encourage each small group to roleplay the situation among themselves, interacting as a family might, *and also* attempting to come to some understanding/solution/resolution as a family unit.

When each small group has completed the roleplay as best they can, tell them to use the evaluation questions at the bottom of RM-2, and discuss how values contributed to the shoplifting incident and also how values contributed to the family's resolution of the situation.

Family Application (5-10 minutes)

Teaching the value of a good spouse.

If what we read earlier in Deuteronomy is correct, then the development of godly values in our children must be more than a one-time shot. Write the following value on the chalkboard: *"A wife [or husband] of noble character . . . is worth far more than rubies"* (Prov. 31:10).

Ask the class participants to suggest as many ways as they can think of that this value can be kept before their children in accord with the instructions in Deuteronomy 6:6-9. Some suggestions might be:

· Have the family help make a poster to display on the parents' wedding anniversary.

· Discuss why *character,* rather than abilities and appearance, is most important.

· Discuss the meaning of "noble."

· Make sure the children overhear both parents expressing appreciation to each other.

· Make sure the children observe both parents treating their spouse with great value.

· Assure the children that they are becoming persons of similar noble character, and value them as such.

· Assure them that if the Lord wills them to get married, they, too, will be able to find a spouse of such high quality.

· Read Proverbs 31 as a family and discuss it.

Encourage the class to notice how many approaches for developing this value in their children depend on relationships and examples of integrity in contrast to the mere statement of the precept.

Wrap-Up (5 minutes)

Briefly summarize the content of this session. Conclude with prayer, thanking God for the privilege of being parents and asking for strength and wisdom in fulfilling this important responsibility.

SESSION 4 · WHAT DO I VALUE?

Objectives—To help people:

· IDENTIFY several personal values.
· SHARE these values with others.
· EVALUATE personal values.
· PLAN which values need changing.
· PRAY for other participants.

Advance Preparation

Have available:
1. A supply of straight pins and pencils for the name tag activity.
2. TR-6 ("Kinds of Values").
3. An overhead projector and screen.
4. A chalkboard or newsprint.
5. Copies of RM-3 ("Coat of Arms"), RM-4 and RM-5 ("Developing Values") in sufficient quantity for your group. Staple RM-4 and RM-5 together.

Getting Started: Name Tag Activity (10-15 minutes)

Be sure to begin with a welcome and a prayer.
Distribute copies of the "Coat of Arms" handout (RM-3) to group members. Guide the group to complete the coat of arms by drawing simple pictures in each of the areas.

Then distribute the straight pins and instruct the people to tear off the coat of arms from the handout and pin it to their clothes on one shoulder or the other.

Allow at least five minutes for the people to stand up, mingle, and discuss with others what they put on their coat of arms name tags.

Exploring Together: Identifying Personal Values (15-20 minutes)

1. Introduction

Briefly review some of the main points discussed in the last session. Highlight some of the ways in which the family is important for healthy development, especially in the moral and spiritual areas.

The experience of this session will be somewhat different; there will be less input and more time devoted to determining each participant's own values at this point.

Before we can discover and implement ways to teach values to our children and young people, we need to be aware of what our own values are and how they affect our attitudes and behaviors.

2. Kinds of Values

According to Dr. Ted Ward, professor and director of the Values Development Education program at Michigan State University, there are at least three different kinds of values. (Display TR-6, "Kinds of Values," as you review this material.)[1]

Preferences

Preferences include our choices of foods, clothing, favorite football teams, and so on. What would be some other examples of preferences? (Allow a few moments for group members to respond.) *These tastes or preferences tell us, as well as people around us, a great deal about ourselves.*

Investments

The kinds of things in which we invest our time and money also tell about what is important to us. What are some examples of ways we invest our time? Our money? (Allow a few moments for group ideas to emerge.) *What do these investments tell us about people's values?*

Notice that we included both time and money. God has given us both time and money and wants us to be good stewards of them. We do have choices regarding how we invest time and our money.

Patterns

As we look at how we invest our time and money, we develop patterns which begin to affect other areas of life.

For example, if people continue to keep all of their money in savings accounts and neglect the needs of others nearby, a pattern of hoarding money and ignoring others is evident. But if people continually ask, "Is this the best use of our time, talents, or money?" the development of a healthy Christian pattern can emerge.

3. Family Values During Childhood

As we learn to help our children develop values, we need to identify what our values were as children and how they have changed in the process of becoming adults. (Distribute copies of "Developing Values" (RM-4 and RM-5).)

We begin by taking ourselves back to our childhoods. During that period, our values probably were similar to those of our parents—values reflected through tastes and preferences, investments of time and money, and patterns of behavior and decision making.

Close your eyes and think back to your earliest days of life. Walk into the childhood home you remember. Look around at the people. What do you see? What was happening? (Pause for a moment or two.) *What do you remember about your parents' values? What was important to your parents?* (Pause.)

Now open your eyes, and complete the first phase of our "Developing Values" activity. (Allow several

minutes for people to complete the first step, which is to identify family values during childhood for each of the suggested areas by marking *C* at the appropriate place on the continuum. Mention again that values were reflected more by attitudes and actions than by words. Point out that there are blank spaces on the second page for any other values they identify.)

4. Values During Adolescence

Now reflect back to your adolescence, the time of life when you grew from being a dependent child, became physically mature, and learned to have deeper relationships with friends and family. For some people, the adolescent years may have been turbulent; for others, they may have been relatively calm. But most of you were involved in a search for identity, a quest for finding out who you were.

Close your eyes again. Think back to the years between ages 12 and 18. Walk into the junior or senior high school you attended. Walk down the hall. Stop and talk with your friends. (Pause.) What was important to you as an adolescent? (Pause.) How important were your friends? Family? Church? (Pause.) What kind of person were you becoming? How did you feel about your physical development and appearance? (Pause.) How did you handle your feelings? (Pause for a few moments.)

Now open your eyes, and complete the second phase of the "Developing Values" activity. (Allow

several minutes for people to complete the next step, which is to identify their own personal values during adolescence. Be sure that persons identify their own developing values and not their family's values for this section. Again, participants place a symbol on each continuum to show how they valued each area.)

5. Values During Adulthood

During the adult years, most of us have intensified our search for who we are, possibly through being married, having children, finding and developing a career. Values continue to be clarified and modified throughout our adult years.

Close your eyes one more time, and reflect on what is happening in your life right now. Briefly think about what a typical day or week is like for you. What are some of your tastes or preferences? Your investments of time and money? Your patterns of decision making? (Pause.) What is really important to you right now—things which are reflected by your attitudes and behaviors and not just your words? (Pause.)

Now open your eyes, and complete the next phase of the "Developing Values" activity, which involves identification of current values. (Allow several minutes for people to complete the next step regarding their current values. Guide participants to put the appropriate symbol on each continuum to show current values.)

Now it is time for us to reflect back on what we

have identified as past and present values. This will also give us opportunity to evaluate where we all are, and to identify any areas we would like to change in the near future.

Sharing Together: Covenant Groups (20-25 minutes)

Guide participants to divide into groups of three or four. Encourage the people to covenant to pray for each other during the coming week about these shared concerns.

Then encourage the groups to share some of the highlights of their development of values from childhood, through adolescence, into adulthood—especially values which have changed.

Ask that participants share any areas they would like to change and then pray for each other. Encourage the people to covenant to pray for each other during the coming week about these shared concerns.

Family Application (5-10 minutes)

Teaching the value of generosity.

This session has concentrated on identifying one's own values at the present time, and yet many of you may have found it significant to see that the roots of some of your most important values go back to your family experiences when you were a child.

Jesus said, "It is more blessed to give than to receive" (Acts 20:35), and this is one of the values which is most effectively developed in children by the practices (and not just the words) of the family.

Consider having a family council meeting to decide which of several Christian relief agencies your family might wish to support. When information on three or four options has been gathered, convene the family meeting, make your selection with everyone having a part in the decision, and figure out how everyone in the family can contribute a portion of the monthly support your family will be sending. Some of the younger children may only contribute a few cents out of their allowance, but it is the involvement, not the amount, which counts.

Receipts for your contributions will often be accompanied by reports from the agency. Don't throw these away as junk mail; take a few moments to read them at the table to help your children realize the blessedness in being able to give to those in need. Some of the agencies which provide support for needy children arrange for periodic personal letters from "your" child overseas.

Wrap-Up (5 minutes

Mention that in the next session, the group will begin to relate this discussion about values and moral development to our Christian faith. Sources of guidance to help us in decision making will be identified. The group will also work together to identify essential Christian values, especially the values of Jesus Christ, and relate these values to our family relationships.

Note
[1]Ted Ward, *Values Begin at Home* (Wheaton, IL: Victor Books, 1979, p. 13ff.

UNIT 2 · HOW FIRM A FOUNDATION?

Focus

God has provided us with a relationship with Jesus Christ, with the Scriptures, the Church, reason, conscience, and the Holy Spirit to guide our decision making.

Scripture Background

Psalm 8:5; Proverbs 9:10; Matthew 21:12, 13; 22:29, 37-40; Mark 2:14, 23-28; Luke 7:36-50; 10:38-42; 18:15-17; 19:1-10; John 2:1-11; 4:14; 14:6; 15:16, 17; 16:12-14; Romans 7:13—8:4; II Corinthians 5:17, 18; Galatians 5:1, 13; Philippians 4:8; I John 3:1, 16, 18; 4:9, 10.

Unit Objectives—To help people:

· IDENTIFY several important sources of guidance for decision making.
· DESCRIBE several essential Christian values.
· RELATE Scriptural teachings to family situations.
· PRAY for God's help in making moral decisions.

For Your Reflection . . .

We live in a world which seems to feel like sinking sand at times—conflicting systems of values, the influence of secular values, confusion as to what is really right or wrong, the pressures and stresses of jobs and family relationships, trying to find a sense of personal identity.

But in the midst of what may feel confusing or overwhelming, if not frightening, we have a solid rock, a firm foundation for coping with life—a dynamic relationship with Jesus Christ. This relationship can provide a grounding or core of security and love which can help us weather any storm or cope with any trauma which may come our way in life.

God has given us several essential sources of guidance for dealing with the great variety of moral decisions with which we are confronted. God's Word is an authoritative guide which gives us many essential Christian values for our use today, and His Spirit continues to live within us, teaching, encouraging, motivating us to do what we find to be the right or best decision.

Unit Highlights

	Getting Started (10-15 minutes)	Exploring Together (15-20 minutes)	Sharing Together (20-25 minutes)	Family Application (5-10 minutes) Teaching the Value of . . .
	Simulation Activity	Sources of Guidance TR-7	Rotating Discussion Groups TR-8	The Bible
	"Jesus" Acrostic	Jesus and Our Values TR-7, 9	Scripture Search RM-6	The Beatitudes
7	Values Graffiti	What Are Essential Christian Values? TR-10	Scripture Search RM-7	Forgiveness
8	Cinquain Poem	What Do I Do When Values Conflict? TR-11	Situations Assessment RM-8	Brotherly Counsel

SESSION 5 · WHAT'S OUR GUIDE?

Objectives—To help people:

· IDENTIFY several basic sources of guidance for decision making.
· DISCUSS the uses and abuses of each source.
· DESCRIBE how each source of guidance can help them in the decision-making process.
· PRAY for wisdom in making moral decisions.

Advance Preparation

Have available:
1. TR-7 ("Sources of Guidance for Christians") and TR-8 ("Rotating Discussion Groups").
2. An overhead projector and screen.
3. A chalkboard or newsprint.
4. Several sheets of blank paper and pencils for use in the Sharing Together activity.

Getting Started: Simulation Activity (10-15 minutes)

Welcome everyone. Ask God to guide the group as together you embark on this study on sources of authority and guidance for Christians.

Ask the group to imagine being in this situation: *You are flying in a small plane with three other people through an unfamiliar area which is mostly wilderness. It is foggy and rainy. The pilot loses his way. Finally, fuel begins to run out. You will have to crash-land. You set down roughly in a field. Everyone survives the crash without injury, but when you get together, you realize that the map has been lost in the crash. You seem to be miles from any town or people. How will you find help? What will you do?*

Divide the large group into groups of four to discuss this situation for a few minutes. Then gather back in the large group to share ideas.

Exploring Together: Sources of Guidance (15-20 minutes)

1. Introduction

Being lost in a new area without a map can be a frightening experience, can't it? Many times when we have to confront a difficult decision, we may have a similar kind of feeling—having to face a complex dilemma without being sure what the right decision should be. We may feel lost and unsure.

Life is full of such dilemmas. Sometimes we may wish we could return to a more simple time in history, perhaps when decisions seemed more clear and less complex.

But God has promised us that He will not forsake us. (See Ps. 94:14.) He knows the situations we are in and clearly wants to guide and help us.

As we face difficult decisions and dilemmas, there are several sources of guidance available to help us. (Option: Brainstorm group ideas as to what these sources might be. Use TR-7, "Sources of Guidance for the Christian," as you review the following material with the group.) *These guides can provide us with principles and values as we make moral decisions.*

2. Jesus Christ As Savior and Lord

As believers, we live in a growing relationship with Jesus Christ. Jesus has told us, "I am the way and the truth and the life. No one comes to the Father except through me" (Jn. 14:6). Jesus has taught us to act in ways which will give witness to God's grace. As we are confronted by sin and evil in the world and make decisions which are less than clear-cut, we act upon our personal relationship with Christ, not upon a system of specific legal ideas.

While we mature as believers, we begin to experience the freedom of the Christian life, freedom from the bonds of sin and self-centeredness. Yet we face a dilemma. Even as we experience freedom in Christ, we may continue to struggle with our weaknesses and sins. In our earthly lives, we may never be totally free. Yet we no longer need to be in bondage to our weaknesses.

Basic to understanding how to be the person Jesus Christ wants each of us to be then, is to follow Jesus and live according to His teachings.

As our relationship with Christ continues to mature, we learn attitudes toward God, others, ourselves, and the world—attitudes based upon God's love rather than only on our personal feelings. We also learn to follow a direction—a call to an exciting life of discipleship.

For the Christian, then, Jesus Christ is at the core of identifying what God's will is for us. And He will illuminate the options and deeply condition our choices.

3. The Scriptures

We also have the Scriptures, which are God's inspired Word. As we live in a sea of rapidly changing traditions and values, the Scriptures can provide us with an anchor.

Yet it seems that God has not intended the Bible to be a code book of laws that would cover every situation. Instead, often the Scriptures give us vital principles which can help us as we work out the specifics in our generation.

The Scriptures set certain standards for how we should think, feel, and act. The Bible helps people understand their need for God and leads them into a dynamic relationship with Him through repentance and faith. Moreover, the Scriptures contain many guidelines to direct us through life, through laws (such as the Ten Commandments), as well as through the moral examples and object lessons found throughout the Old and New Testaments.

The Scriptures remind us that we cannot discover God or His will through reason alone. The Holy Spirit will guide us to understand and implement the teachings of Scripture. (See Jn. 16:13, 14.)

One of the most difficult tasks is to distinguish between what is eternal and what probably was intended to apply specifically to the times in which the Scriptures were written. In this situation, it is important to allow the New Testament to interpret the Old, so that we can have an overall view of what God intended to teach in His Word.

4. Traditions and Church Teachings

Through the centuries, after the time when the Scriptures were written, many traditions have developed which have identified values. Some traditions (such as those guiding churches to know how to organize themselves and function, policies regarding the importance of marriage, and so on) have lasted for centuries. But other traditions (often regarding specific behaviors) seem more appropriate to one time than another.

What would be an example of a church tradition which was not permanent? (Ask for an example or two. In some churches, for example, the wearing of makeup or nylon stockings was unacceptable for a period of time; later these traditions may have changed.)

And that is one difficulty in using church traditions as permanent laws: such traditions are often influenced by the times and cultural customs in which they originated. We need to evaluate such traditions constantly in light of what we understand the Scriptures to be teaching us and in light of our growing relationship with Jesus Christ.

5. Reason

People not only have senses; they can also think logically and organize their feelings and sense perceptions in logical ways.

Common sense is critical for establishing values and making moral decisions, but reason can also be misused. It can be tempting for us to rationalize any act or value.

What would be an example of a person or situation in which reason was misused? (Have participants share an example or two. Ideas: the Pharisees' lack of understanding regarding why Jesus had come; Adolf Hitler's feelings and actions toward the Jewish people; rationalizing feelings of racial hatred; and so on.)

As important as reasoning is, we need to acknowledge that our needs and feelings affect our ability to think clearly and objectively and so influence our values and moral decisions.

(If possible, share a personal experience when your reasoning was heavily influenced by your needs or feelings. Or, ask if a class member could share such an experience.)

6. Conscience

Another source of guidance we all have is our consciences. The conscience is an inner voice which arouses feelings regarding the rightness or wrongness of certain actions.

For children, conscience is often a sense of "mustness" which involves the fear of punishment if something wrong is done. For the developing adolescent and adult, the conscience becomes a sense of "oughtness."

In the book The Individual and His Religion, Gordon Allport describes conscience as "the knife-edge that all our values press upon us whenever we are acting, or have acted, contrary to these values."[1]

An important question for us to ask is this: Do our consciences always tell us what is really right? Are these feelings of unsettledness or guilt always appropriate? (Take a few moments for people to respond to these questions.)

These are questions with which people have struggled for centuries. We do need to acknowledge that our consciences are affected by our culture and by the conditioning we experience in our growing-up years.

That is why some people may feel guilty about certain situations, while other people may not have such feelings. Again, we need to measure the feelings our consciences arouse by the teachings of Scripture and the leading of the Holy Spirit.

The Scriptures tell us that the problem with doing what is right is often not a problem of adequate knowledge, but of courage to put into action what we have already seen as right or good. It may be a problem of will. (See Rom. 7:13—8:4 for a description of Paul's dilemma with these conflicts.)

At the same time, we need to listen to this inner voice of conscience. To repress or ignore the conscience is to feel tormented and troubled inwardly.

7. The Holy Spirit

Another vital source of guidance is the Holy Spirit. The Scriptures tell us that the Holy Spirit is an inexhaustible spring of living water welling up within the Christian. (See Jn. 4:14; 7:38, 39.)

The Bible teaches us that the Holy Spirit is a teacher, a guide, a source of moral strength who gives not only enlightenment, but also the desire and courage to follow what is good and true. (See Jn. 16:12-14.)

The Holy Spirit motivates us to love and is inseparably bound to our relationship with Jesus Christ.

Even as we acknowledge the importance of the Holy Spirit in our lives, we need to be careful that the leadings or urgings we feel are tested against the teachings of Scripture. There needs to be a balance between the objective teachings which our reasoning helps us perceive and the subjective, inner feelings which we have.

Sharing Together: Rotating Discussion Groups (20-25 minutes)

Move the chairs into five circles of approximately equal size. Display TR-8 ("Rotating Discussion Groups") and cover up Phase II. Mention that the participants will now have opportunity to discuss these sources of guidance in more detail.

List the options for Phase I, and identify in which circle of chairs each option will be discussed. Then have participants move to the circle of their choice. Ask them to make a second choice if the group of their first choice is already full, so that the groups remain approximately the same size. Ask for a volunteer in each group to jot down the group's ideas, and then let the discussion begin.

After five to eight minutes in groups, have the recorders from each small group share their thoughts, briefly, in the larger group.

Then refer again to TR-8 with Phase II now uncovered. Again, identify where the five topics will each be discussed, and repeat the same process as with Phase I.

Family Application (5-10 minutes)

Teaching the value of the Bible.
"Your word is a lamp to my feet and a light for my path" (Ps. 119:105). *How can we as parents help to develop within our children an appreciation of the value of God's Word?*

The first step is to ask what is the light to your feet and a guide to your path? And do your children know that about you? It may not be enough for your children to simply know that you have devotions, if you do; it is also important for them to know why you have them. And one of the reasons is to discover God's direction for your life.

The next time you face a moral decision, share it with your children if it is not over their heads. Then let them know how you arrive at your answer after considering God's Word. If this is a difficult choice you contemplate for several days, let them in on the process and ask for their prayers. If it is a simple matter to which you know the godly answer without much thought, share that as well, and mention the Scriptures you recall as relevant.

Be sure you show your children your values as well as tell them. Actually, you won't be able to hide what's really there, but you can draw special attention to it.

Parents too often hide their moral struggles and general decisions from their children more than is necessary. There are actually only two cautions: don't burden a child with a confidence he or she cannot easily keep or information which might be frightening or too heavy for them; and don't lay any responsibility for making your decision upon a child. Certainly the child's age and maturity are relevant to these two cautions.

Wrap-Up (5 minutes

Acknowledge that this session has dealt with some heavy concepts. But it is hoped that identifying and clarifying the sources of guidance we have as believers can help us make the kinds of moral decisions that are right or best in particular situations.

Conclude with prayer, asking God for wisdom in using these sources of guidance prudently as we seek to become the people and families God wants us to be.

Note
[1]Gordon Allport, *The Individual and His Religion* (New York: The Macmillan Company, 1962), p. 90.

SESSION 6 · JESUS AND VALUES

bjectives—To help people:

· DESCRIBE Jesus' influence upon their values.
· READ selected Scriptures which describe Jesus' values through His teachings and example.
· LIST values Jesus espoused.
· RELATE Jesus' values to everyday family situations.

dvance Preparation

Have available:
1. Several sheets of newsprint, felt pens, and masking tape, for the Getting Started activity.
2. TR-7 ("Sources of Guidance for Christians") and TR-9 ("Jesus Christ and Our Values").
3. An overhead projector and screen.
4. Copies of RM-6 ("Jesus and Values") in sufficient quantity so that every participant will have a copy.
5. A chalkboard or newsprint.
6. Several Bibles for the Sharing Together activity.

etting Started: "Jesus" crostic (10-15 minutes)

Begin by welcoming participants to this session. Pray that God will deepen your understanding and motivate everyone to do what is right.

Divide into several smaller groups. Give each small group a sheet of newsprint and a felt pen. Instruct groups to print the following letters down the length of the sheet: J-E-S-U-S—C-H-R-I-S-T. (See sketch.)

```
J
E
S
U
S

C
H
R
I
S
T
```

Ask groups to develop an acrostic by thinking of words which begin with each of these letters and which describe Jesus or how group members feel about Jesus.

After groups have completed their acrostics, tape them around the room. Ask a representative from each group to read the words listed on each acrostic.

Exploring Together: Jesus and Our Values (15-20 minutes)

1. Introduction

Briefly review the content of the previous session by displaying TR-7 ("Sources of Guidance for the Christian") and summarizing the sources of guidance God has provided us as we make moral decisions. Emphasize that for the believer, Jesus Christ and our relationship with Him is central to any consideration of values.

There are three basic ways that Jesus Christ influences our values and moral decisions: Our relationship with Him, His teachings, and His example. (Use TR-9, "Jesus Christ and Our Values," as you present this material.)

2. Our Relationship with Jesus Christ

Basic to our faith is our relationship with Jesus Christ. There is more to our faith than a listing of beliefs in a creed, as important as such beliefs are. Being a Christian involves the acknowledgment of Jesus as our Savior and Lord.

And this relationship should not be static or casual. Any relationship which is neglected or ignored will become more cool or distant. Relationships need nurturing and attention. And this is especially true regarding our relationship with Jesus Christ.

How does a relationship with Christ grow? (Ask for group ideas. Thoughts: through study, prayer, being involved in ministries which stretch our faith, obedience, and so on. Write responses on chalkboard or newsprint.)

What can stifle the growth of our relationship with Christ? (Ask for group ideas. Thoughts: lack of interest, other priorities, etc. Write responses on chalkboard or newsprint.)

3. The Teachings of Jesus

"Rabbi," or "Teacher," was an important title Jesus had in His years on earth. And He continues to be our Teacher today, through His teachings recorded in the Scriptures.

Jesus spent most of His earthly years teaching people about who He is, how we can be related to Him, and how we as believers should act in relationship to others. The Scriptures give us many

We find that Jesus Christ was also lovable. He appreciated and gratefully accepted the love expressed by others. (For example, see Lk. 7:36-50.)

Yet Jesus could be angry when appropriate. We find that Jesus was often angry with the Pharisees, those people who tried so hard to have all of the right answers and were so judgmental in their attitudes regarding others. (Mt. 21:12, 13; Lk. 7:39.)

And Jesus was not afraid to confront complex moral issues in which two or more values seemed to conflict. (See Mk. 2:23-28 as an example.)

Jesus consistently measured His words, attitudes, and actions by what God the Father wanted for Him. (See Jn. 5:19-24.)

We see that Jesus' way of handling moral conflicts was one of grateful, loyal response to God. In contrast, the Pharisees and others saw a burdening sense of obligation as guiding their moral decision making; a burden so heavy that it suffocated the very relationship they sought to maintain with God.

5. Conclusion

As we are confronted by complex decisions, especially regarding values or moral concerns, we need to keep our relationship with Jesus Christ, His teachings and His example, at the core of who we are and who we are becoming.

Sharing Together: Scriptur Search (20-25 minutes

Distribute copies of the "Jesus and Values" handout (RM-6). Briefly describe the process to be used in this activity. Depending upon your available time, have small groups study several or all references, or assign one or two references to each group so that all Scriptures are studied.

Guide the group to look up the Scripture references and read the verses.

Then the participants will identify what can be learned by Jesus' teachings and by His example in each of these narratives concerning values.

Encourage groups to think of at least one family situation in which each of these teachings can be helpful.

As time permits, share back in the large group.

Family Application (5-1 minutes

Teaching the values in the Beatitudes.
"Blessed are the merciful . . . pure in heart . . . peacemakers . . ." (Mt. 5:7-12). Each of the Beatitudes are statements of value by Jesus. The word

basic guidelines for dealing with life, such as the Sermon on the Mount in Matthew 5, 6, and 7.

What are some of the teachings of Jesus which have been particularly helpful or meaningful to you? (Allow a few moments for participants to respond. Be sure to share an example or two of your own.)

4. The Example of Jesus

Jesus taught not only with His words. He also taught us important truths through His example— the way He related to various people, the expressions of His feelings and attitudes about certain people and ideas, and so on.

(We will see in a subsequent session how powerfully our own example teaches our children, for better or worse.)

Jesus is the greatest and most authoritative Example of the kinds of values and beliefs, as well as attitudes and actions, which we should imitate.

We see that Jesus was gentle, loving, and compassionate. He loved children and party celebrations. (See Lk. 18:15-17; Jn. 2:1-11.) Yet He invested great amounts of His energy in teaching others, whether as individuals or in groups. He was always available to teach and minister.

And Jesus was particularly loving to people who had blatantly sinned against God or failed others. (See Jn. 8:3-11; Lk. 19:1-10; Jn. 4 as examples.)

blessed, *which begins each one, means how fortunate, how happy, or how desirable it is—clear expressions of value. But how do we develop these values in our children when we find the characteristics so hard to cultivate within ourselves?*

Our children can learn from our failures as well as our successes. What we are after in developing values is a hunger and a thirst for the things God prizes. A poor person can value money as highly as a rich one. And just so, we can value qualities we have not yet mastered.

In terms of the Beatitudes, what are the qualities we admire? Ruthlessness or mercifulness? Being macho or a peacemaker?

The way to cultivate values within our children which go beyond the behaviors we can consistently produce is to use confession. *James offers us this key: "Confess your sins to each other and pray for each other" (Jas. 5:16).*

So, the next time you display failure to live out the very Beatitudes you value, use that occasion to sit down with your family and confess that failure, and ask them to pray for you. You will have taken one great step in communicating how important that value is, and it will be contagious.

Also, the fact that you fail in the very things you value will teach your children how to cope with failure and then move on—a most important lesson.

Wrap-Up (5 minutes)

Ask several participants to conclude with prayer, thanking God for His loving care and for the support and help we obtain through the life and teachings of Jesus Christ. Ask God for guidance in translating these understandings into workable attitudes and behaviors in our families.

SESSION 7 · WHAT ARE ESSENTIAL CHRISTIAN VALUES?

Objectives—To help people:

· STATE several essential Christian values.
· DIFFERENTIATE between Christian and secular values.
· RELATE Christian values to family concerns.

Advance Preparation

Have available:
1. A large sheet of newsprint or butcher paper (at least three feet by six feet) with lettering as shown in sketch:

CHRISTIAN VALUES	SECULAR VALUES

2. Crayons or felt pens for the Getting Started activity.
3. TR-10 ("Essential Christian Values").
4. An overhead projector and screen.
5. Copies of RM-7 ("Christian Values")—one copy for each participant.
6. A chalkboard or newsprint.
7. Several Bibles for the Sharing Together activity.

Getting Started: Values Graffiti (10-15 minutes)

As people arrive, direct them to the area where you have taped the sheet of newsprint and have them identify various values in the two sections marked "Christian Values" and "Secular Values" and to do one of the following:
· Write the word or words describing the value (whether Christian or secular) in the appropriate section.
· Write a phrase or sentence describing the value.
· Draw a picture of a family situation in which a particular value would be evident.

Encourage as many people as possible to make a contribution to the "Values" graffiti.

As you begin this session, take a few moments to highlight some of the contributions people have made describing Christian and secular values. Ask God for wisdom for yourself and every participant in discussing these important matters regarding Christian values.

Exploring Together: What Are Essential Christian Values (15-20 minutes)

1. Introduction

Briefly review a few of the key thoughts of the past two sessions:

God has provided several sources of guidance for us as we make moral decisions. (Guide group to identify all six sources: relationship with Jesus Christ, Scriptures, traditions and church teachings, reason, conscience, and the Holy Spirit.)

Jesus Christ can guide us to become maturing Christians as we develop a growing relationship with Him.

We also learn about important Christian values by studying the teachings and example of Jesus as recorded in the Scriptures.

We could spend many weeks exploring the great number of values which the Scriptures teach. But in this particular session, we will focus on several general values which can influence more specific dilemmas and decisions. (Refer to TR-10, "Essential Christian Values," as you share the following material with your group.)

2. God-centered

The goal of our lives as human beings is to enjoy and glorify God in whatever we think, say, feel, or do. The Scriptures tell us, "The fear of the Lord is the beginning of wisdom, and knowledge of the Holy One is understanding" (Prov. 9:10).

Jesus taught us to respond to God with gratitude and love because of His love for us—love which has been personalized through Jesus Christ. Our relationship with God is primarily one of love, not wrath, and Christ is the embodiment of this love. (See II Cor. 5:17, 18.)

We know that God is active in all events in life. And no matter what happens, God does provide us with the resources of grace for confronting the difficult as well as the joyous experiences of life.

This vertical relationship between ourselves and God must be at the core of any consideration of values. We need to ask ourselves constantly: Do our actions reflect our love for God?

Our love for God brings us into a relationship which gradually transforms and renews our temperaments, personalities, attitudes, behaviors, and values. The Scriptures describe in great detail the kinds of personal qualities which God values for us.

The apostle Paul reminds us, "Finally, brothers, whatever is true, whatever is noble, whatever is right, whatever is pure, whatever is lovely, whatever is admirable—if anything is excellent or praiseworthy—think about such things" (Phil. 4:8).

Believers are called to be meek, merciful, pure in heart, peacemakers. (See Mt. 5:3-9.)

We are freed from the bondage of self-centeredness and from anxiety about being accepted by others or about our future. (See Gal. 5:1, 13.)

3. Concerned with Persons

Our relationship with God—the vertical dimension— affects both our feelings about ourselves and our relationship with other people—the horizontal dimension. The two dimensions are inseparable. (Refer to the illustration of the principle on TR-10, "Essential Christian Values.")

It is God who has initiated love with us. Our response needs to be one of faith, humility, appreciation, and love for those around us.

Jesus has told us, " 'Love your neighbor as yourself.' All the Law and the Prophets hang on these two commandments" (Mt. 22:39, 40).

People are important to God. In fact, in the earliest chapters of Scripture, we are reminded that we have been made in God's image, not only in our ability to reason and have feelings and values, but also in our ability to be related personally to God. (See Ps. 8:5.)

And God felt that people were so important that He gave the very best that He had—His only Son Jesus—to be the means through which people could be reconciled with God after their sins had cut them off from Him. We all are sinners, but we can be reconciled through Christ to God. (See Rom. 5:8.)

4. The Primacy of Love

The key word in all of our consideration of Christian values is love. The Scriptures talk not of a self-regarding love, but a self-giving love. (See I Jn. 3:16, 18; 4:9, 10.) It is the kind of love which seeks to satisfy the other person in a relationship without thought of reward or benefit to self.

So the moral person is one who loves, who is growing in the ability to love others unconditionally, without the strings we can so easily attach to our relationships (e.g., "I can love you if . . . . I will love you when . . . .").

Yet, the love we share with others also recognizes the importance of self-respect and love. Loving others does not mean that we hate ourselves. Rather, according to Christ, we love others as we grow in our acceptance and love for ourselves. (See Lk. 10:27.)

This kind of self-love is quite different from self-centered love, conceit, or pride. A Christian perspective on self-love is that it involves a realistic appraisal of oneself—including one's strengths and weaknesses and sins. Pride or conceit, on the other hand, denies or represses the negative parts of ourselves and seeks to dominate or manipulate others.

What are some characteristics of Christian love? (Take a few moments to brainstorm. Write down the group's ideas on chalkboard or newsprint. Be sure the following ideas are included: a willingness to listen and be involved with people, to accept others as they are, to treat them with respect, justice, being lovable, and so on.)

5. Conclusion

We have identified several essential Christian values, including the centrality of God, concern for people, and the primacy of love. We have both the privilege and the responsibility, in turn, to relate these general values to very specific situations— and our families are the most important place to begin.

Sharing Together: Scripture Search (20-25 minutes)

Distribute copies of the "Christian Values" handout (RM-7). The process to be used in this activity is similar to that used in the previous session. Again, depending upon your available time, have small groups study several or all Scripture references, or assign one section or reference to each group. The selections being used for this study are the Ten Commandments (Ex. 20:2-17), and Paul's words regarding the fruits of the Spirit (Gal. 5:22, 23).

Guide the participants to identify the values being described, as well as family situations where these values could be particularly helpful. As time permits, share back in the large group.

Family Application (5-10 minutes)

Teaching the value of forgiveness.

Forgiveness is one of the most central Christian values. Jesus said, "If you forgive men when they sin against you, your heavenly Father will also forgive you" (Mt. 6:14). Cultivating within our children a sense of the usefulness and importance of forgiveness has at least two essential benefits.

The first benefit is relational. Forgiveness is one

of the most important transactions in the process of reconciliation. When a break happens between two people, it is finally bridged when forgiveness is pronounced. (Other essential steps include confession and repentance.) When forgiveness is not pronounced, distance between people may linger in uncertainty. "Are things really okay? Or is he still mad at me?"

The other benefit is that forgiveness deals with guilt. Many people struggle with feelings of guilt throughout their lives even after they have repented and asked God's forgiveness. One of the reasons is often that they have not grown up in an environment where forgiveness was transacted. If others have not formally forgiven them, how can they be sure God has truly forgiven them?

The value of forgiveness can be taught in the family most effectively by practicing it. To some people it may seem awkward at first to wait for or elicit the specific words, "I forgive you," to end a matter. It is so much more common to dismiss an apology by saying, "It's okay," "Forget it," "It was nothin'." But it was something, and everybody knows it. Telling children that they are forgiven, or helping them say it to one another or to you when resolving an offense, is one of the best ways to teach this Christian value. And they will be able to believe that God forgives them, too.

Wrap-Up (5 minute

Summarize key thoughts from this session. Ask several participants to read verses from a current paraphrase of I Corinthians 13. Then conclude with a time of conversational prayer, in which individuals are encouraged to pray short prayers regarding specific concerns related to Christian values and their families.

SESSION 8 · WHAT DO I DO WHEN VALUES CONFLICT?

Objectives—To help people:

· DIFFERENTIATE between Christian and secular values.
· LIST criteria for identifying Christian values.
· ASSESS conflicting values in selected family situations.

Advance Preparation

Have available:

1. A large sheet of newsprint, or a chalkboard, on which you write the following directions, as shown in sketch:

WRITING A CINQUAIN POEM ABOUT VALUES

Line 1: Theme word.
Line 2: Two words that describe the theme word.
Line 3: Three words to describe some action related to the theme word. (Often "ing" words are used.)
Line 4: Four words that describe your feelings about the theme word.
Line 5: Another name for the theme word, or use the theme word again.

Write your words in the pattern shown below.

        _____   _____

    _____   _____   _____

_____   _____   _____   _____

_____ _____   _____   _____

          _____

---

2. Write a sample cinquain poem. (See Getting Together time for suggestions.)
3. TR-11, "Christian Values Versus Secular Values."
4. An overhead projector and screen.
5. Copies of RM-8 ("Conflicting Values")—one copy for each participant.
6. A chalkboard or newsprint tablet.

Getting Together: Cinquain Poem (10-15 minutes)

Welcome everyone and mention that this is the last session in the second unit. Thank God for this opportunity to learn about values and the family.

Point out the directions for the "Cinquain Poem on Values" activity. Brainstorm several ideas for theme words. (Ideas: values, conflict, right, wrong, family, children, parents.) Guide them to complete the activity. People can work individually or in small groups. If possible, write a poem before the session and share it as a sample.

Example:

Values
Important, Helpful
Clarifying, Judging, Developing
Positive, Negative, Ambivalent, Hopeful
Values

Encourage as many people as possible to share their poems in the group.

Exploring Together: What Do I Do When Values Conflict? (10-15 minutes)

1. Introduction

Briefly review key thoughts from the previous three sessions:

· Sources of guidance for Christians include: relationship with Christ, Scriptures, traditions and church teachings, reason, conscience, and the Holy Spirit.
· What we identified as essential Christian values: being God-centered, concern for persons, the primacy of love, and so on.

One of the dilemmas which face us is that decisions are not always clear-cut, but seem to be in a gray area between right and wrong. And, in some situations, we seem to be choosing between the lesser of evils (called a "tragic moral choice").

An example of such a dilemma would be the decision of whether or not to stay with a spouse who has had repeated affairs in recent years. What are the issues involved? What would be the better choice? (Briefly discuss together.)

A more extreme example would be: You are driving a school bus filled with children through the mountains. The brakes on the bus fail as you approach a busy picnic area. Your choices are: go over the edge of a mountain cliff, or run into an area filled with elderly people. What would be the better choice? (Briefly discuss together.)

2. Christian Values Versus Secular Values

One of our dilemmas as Christians is that we are surrounded on every side by conflicting values which are not God-centered. (Refer to TR-11, "Christian Values Versus Secular Values.") *What would be examples of secular values?* Brainstorm ideas as a group. Be sure the following are included:

· Materialism—the worship of possessions and things.

· Narcissism—Me-first, or "I want it NOW"; self-gratification at the expense of others.

· Atheism—or Godlessness.

Often times these secular values seem quite subtle. Yet their potency is apparent everywhere.

The apostle Paul describes the qualities which are evident in secular values (what he calls "the works of the flesh"): "Sexual immorality, impurity and debauchery; idolatry and witchcraft; hatred, discord, jealousy, fits of rage, selfish ambition, dissensions, factions and envy; drunkenness, orgies, and the like" (Gal. 5:19-21).

As Christians surrounded by pressures such as those described by the Scriptures, we may have many different feelings. (Briefly share examples: feeling overwhelmed, threatened, angry, afraid, and so on.)

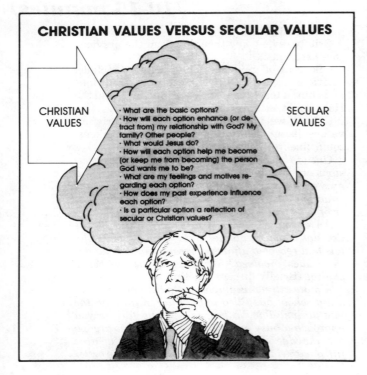

CHRISTIAN VALUES VERSUS SECULAR VALUES

CHRISTIAN VALUES

SECULAR VALUES

· What are the basic options?
· How will each option enhance (or detract from) my relationship with God? My family? Other people?
· What would Jesus do?
· How will each option help me become (or keep me from becoming) the person God wants me to be?
· What are my feelings and motives regarding each option?
· How does my past experience influence each option?
· Is a particular option a reflection of secular or Christian values?

3. Dealing with the "Grays" of Life

As we deal with issues in which there seem to be gray areas between absolute right or wrong, we need to honestly face questions such as (refer to TR-11, "Christian Values Versus Secular Values," as you list questions):

· *What are the basic options in this situation?*

· *How will each option enhance (or detract from) my relationship with God? my family? other people?*

· *What would Jesus do if He were in this situation?*

· *How will each option help me become (or keep me from becoming) the person God wants me to be?*

· *What are my feelings and motives regarding each option?*

· *How do my past experiences (previous teachings, attitudes of others, and so on) influence each option?*

· *Is a particular option a reflection of secular or Christian values?*

(Ask the group to identify any other questions which should be asked when faced with moral dilemmas.)

What kinds of things can affect our abilities to make clear-cut moral decisions? Ask group for their ideas. List them on chalkboard or newsprint as they brainstorm. Be sure the following are included:

Lack of time for reflection

Quality of a relationship (for example, the effects of a poor husband-wife or parent-child relationship)

Poor previous experience

Lack of understanding or maturity

Poor self-esteem and self-respect

Being "out of touch" with God (unconfessed sin, mixed-up priorities, and so on).

4. Decision Making and Other Factors

As we have already mentioned, our perplexities do not always result because of a lack of knowledge. Instead, as the apostle Paul mentions, our problem may be:

A problem of the WILL. (See Rom. 7:13—8:4.)

A need for COURAGE to put into action what we have already seen as right or good.

A RIGHT ATTITUDE—seeking to do what will honor God with our feelings, attitudes, actions, and values.

5. Conclusion

Some moral decisions are clear-cut and obvious. Others are less clear and are difficult, if not painful.

Author T. S. Eliot spoke of the meaninglessness of human life when he said, "Here were decent godless people. Their only monument the asphalt road and a thousand lost golf balls."

Hopefully, people who live in subsequent generations will find our morality more memorable than did T.S. Eliot. Our prayer can be that our children and our children's children will remember that we were God-honoring people who kept Christ as the focus of our lives and sought diligently to live according to the timeless principles provided us by the Scriptures. Let us strive to be examples of people who lived by our reason and consciences, were guided by the Holy Spirit, and were both morally and spiritually mature.

Sharing Together: Situations Assessment (20-25 minutes)

Distribute copies of the "Conflicting Values" handout (RM-8). Divide into small groups. Depending upon your available time, either have the small groups discuss as many situations as they can, or assign one or two situations to each group.

You may want to take the first situation and complete the exercise together in the large group to be sure the process is clear. Ask group members to identify the conflicting values. (Ideas on the first situation: wanting to honor and please parents, being concerned about the parent's need for professional care, impact of having an ailing person in your home, and so on.)

Encourage people while they are still in small groups to share any dilemmas they are currently facing in their families and to pray for each other.

Be sure to allow time to share responses back in the larger group.

Family Application (5-10 minutes)

Teaching the value of Christian counsel.

Sorting out moral dilemmas can be a lonely and frightening experience unless we value and make use of the counsel of our brothers and sisters in the Body of Christ. Proverbs 11:14 refers specifically to such hard choices: "Where no counsel is, the people fall: but in the multitude of counsellors there is safety" (KJV). The insights of other caring people can help us see aspects and implications of a problem that we have overlooked. Their experiences may be instructive to us.

Frequently, as children enter adolescence, parents bemoan the fact that their children no longer value or listen to their counsel. But adolescence is the time children begin "trying on" adulthood. If the example of the parents has been to avoid or ignore the counsel of other Christians and to conceal their problems, their children will treat them the same way.

Do you want your children to value your counsel, the counsel of the pastor, or other mature, and caring believers? Then set the example. Share with your Christian brothers and sisters, possibly in a small group committed to seek God and stick with each other through the consequences. Then let your family know that you are paying serious attention to the input from the Body as you make your decision.

In a situation where the family is divided, such as number eight on RM-8, "Conflicting Values," consider inviting the pastor or other mature leaders in your church to sit down with your family to talk through the differences. You might be surprised at the help which results.

Your children will get the point: Growing up doesn't mean reaching an age when one ignores the advice of other, trustworthy believers. And they won't ignore you so quickly, either.

Wrap-Up (5 minutes)

We have pinpointed one of the most difficult issues related to morality and values: What do we do when values conflict, or when Christian values are pressured by secular values?

Knowledge is important, but it is not enough. We need to ask God to motivate us, to give us the courage to act upon what we know to be true, good, or right.

Close with prayer, asking God to fill each person with the love and courage to confront and deal with the moral dilemmas of life.

UNIT 3 · TEACHING VALUES IN THE FAMILY

Focus

God has given parents the opportunity to teach values, both formally and informally, in our families, and to be examples of what we value.

Scripture Background

Proverbs 1:8; 4:1-4; Micah 6:8; Matthew 19:13-15; Luke 6:40.

Unit Objectives—*To help people:*

· DESCRIBE the importance of the home environment for healthy moral development.
· PLAN ways to enhance their home environments.
· IDENTIFY several values-oriented activities they would like to do with their families.
· PRACTICE a method of resolving differences in the family.
· THANK God for love, wisdom, and courage.

For Your Reflection . . .

When we think of teaching values, or guiding the development of values in our families, we may envision the structured teaching which is done in some families, a style in which parents plan and lead activities at home. Perhaps this is appealing to you, or maybe you feel uncomfortable or unsure about this leadership style.

But there is much more to guiding the development of values in the family. *Home environment* is the key. How does the environment in your family facilitate the development of values? Is it loving? Empathic? Just? Intellectually stimulating?

Being an example is a powerful way to teach. Take a few moments to think about the influence of your own example. How do your attitudes and actions influence people around you? How can your example be a positive influence upon the people involved in this learning experience?

As has already been mentioned, Jesus used the power of His example frequently to illustrate and teach many essential lessons to people. How can your example be used by God to illustrate what you are trying to teach?

God has promised to help you be the person He wants you to be—the kind of teacher and facilitator who lovingly exemplifies essential values—through what you say, the attitudes you convey, and the actions that communicate God's loving care to others.

Unit Highlights

Session	Getting Started (10-15 minutes)	Exploring Together (15-20 minutes)	Sharing Together (20-25 minutes)	Family Application (5-19 minutes) Teaching the Value of
9	Prioritizing Responsibilities RM-9	Enhancing the Home Environment TR-12	Fishbowl/Roleplay Discussion	Respect for the Elderly
10	Neighbor Nudge	Being an Example TR-13	Communication Exercise RM-10	Family Unity
11	Brainstorming	Teaching in the Family TR-14	Sharing and Planning RM-11	Courage
12	Multiple Choice Discussion	Working Through Differences TR-15; RM-12	Case Studies RM-13	Peaceful Resolutions
13	Sentence Completion Exercise RM-14	Looking Back, Looking Forward RM-15	Celebration RM-16; TR-16	God's Creation

SESSION 9 · ENHANCING THE HOME ENVIRONMENT

Objectives—To help people:

· RATE the importance of various parenting responsibilities.
· DESCRIBE characteristics of open and closed families.
· IDENTIFY how the home environment can be loving, empathic, just, and intellectually stimulating.
· PLAN ways to improve one's home environment.

Advance Preparation

Have available:
1. Copies of RM-9 ("Responsibilities of Parenting")—one copy for each participant.
2. TR-12 ("Values and the Home Environment").
3. An overhead projector and screen.
4. A chalkboard or newsprint.
5. Four volunteers (two to roleplay parents, two to roleplay adolescents) for the Sharing Together activity.
6. A sheet of blank paper, envelope, and pencil for each participant for the Sharing Together activity.

Getting Started: Prioritizing Responsibilities (10-15 minutes)

Welcome everyone. Mention that with this session you are launching into the third unit of this course, a look at specific ways to teach values in the family. Pray that God will provide wisdom in discerning ways to teach values.

Distribute copies of the "Responsibilities of Parenting" handout (RM-9). Guide people to complete the activity according to the directions provided on the handout.

Once participants have completed ranking the various responsibilities of parenting by importance, divide into small groups of three or four. Have people share their priorities and reasons for them. Then encourage groups to talk until they agree on what the top two responsibilities should be for parents.

Reassemble in the large group. Have a representative from each small group list their top two priorities of parenting. Encourage discussion as to why various priorities were seen as most important.

There is no need to seek consensus from the entire group during this discussion. Mention that parents probably fulfill all of these roles at various times during the typical week.

Exploring Together: Enhancing the Home Environment (15-20 minutes)

1. Introduction
As we think about the importance of the home environment, we need to remember that over a period of time, every family tends to develop certain patterns of interaction or communication. These patterns help families deal with the various kinds of stress—whether from outside the family (such as a job change, depression, a war, and so on), or stress and change from within the family (such as the birth of a child, the death of a parent, the onset of adolescence for one child, the children leaving home, and so on).

2. Open and Closed Families
Family researchers have found that there are two basic kinds of families: open and closed. Remember that families are not usually open or closed exclusively, but may be somewhere in between. (Refer to the illustration at the top of TR-12, "Values and the Home Environment.")

Open families are concerned about the self-worth of each of their members. They deal realistically with stresses and changes. In fact, change is welcomed and considered normal and a sign of growth. Close, loving relationships are highly valued within the family.

Closed families, on the other hand, focus more on power and performance than self-worth. There is often resistance to change. Communication patterns are often indirect and not very clear in closed families. For example, parents in a closed family may talk "through" a child, rather than talking directly to each other.

The main point we want to make is that in open families, healthy relationships tend to exist, parents and children work at living together happily, stresses and changes are dealt with openly.

But achieving this kind of open family is not particularly easy, is it? What kinds of factors may make an open family relationship difficult? (Encourage group to respond. Ideas: poor example from our own parents, resistance from children, excessive stresses, and so on.)
Family counselor Virginia Satir, in her book Peoplemaking, *says this about being a parent:*

I regard this as the hardest, most complicated, anxiety-ridden, sweat-and-blood producing job in the world. It requires the ultimate in patience, common sense, commitment, humor, tact, love, wisdom, awareness, and knowledge. At the same time, it holds the possibility for the most rewarding, joyous experience of a lifetime.[1]

And when we consider the development of Christian values, the environment of the home—the atmosphere or quality of relationships—often teaches more strongly than does direct teaching. And the environment's impact may have a deeper, more lasting influence as well.
Christian educator Catherine M. Stonehouse, in her book Patterns in Moral Development, *maintains that the home environment is very important:*

Some of the most important things in life are learned from the environment in which we live, without any direct teaching. Few people would set out to teach a child that he is stupid, a bother, and unimportant. But when adults insist on doing things for the child, fail to praise his accomplishments, deride him for his failings, sigh when he wants something, and never have time for him, the child learns the lesson well.[2]

Several qualities of the Christian home environment should be our goal: an environment which is loving, empathic, just, and intellectually stimulating. Let's look at each of these qualities in more detail. (Use TR-12, "Values and the Home Environment," as you review the following material.)

3. Providing a LOVING Home Environment

Studies show that a warm and loving parent is imitated more than an unloving parent. And children who live in a positive, accepting environment are more willing to learn and generally more positive and confident than children living in a hostile or frightening environment.

Children who have positive self-esteem are usually from homes where they feel loved, wanted, and appreciated.

This bond of love encourages maturity in moral development, since children are guided more by an inner sense of what should be done than by an external pressure to do something because of the promise of reward or the threat of punishment.

Learning to give overt expressions of love through words and actions, as well as providing quality attention for each child, seems to have lifelong impact. For in being loved, children develop the emotional security and confidence to make deci-

sions on their own. Moreover, the accepting parent provides a positive model with whom children can identify and desire to imitate.

Children who do not receive such love and affirmation, on the other hand, often are driven by unfulfilled emotional needs and pent-up hostility.

4. Providing an EMPATHIC Home Environment

Webster defines empathy as "the capacity for participation in another's feelings or ideas." So the morally maturing person is one who has a developing awareness of the feelings and needs of others. There is a sensitivity to the consequences for others, of one's personal behavior.

Many researchers maintain that empathy can be developed at a fairly young age. Very early in life, a person can begin to understand the difference between accidental and intentional acts.

Parents can talk with their children about the effects their behavior has on the family. And parents can guide children in making decisions by encouraging them to consider the feelings of others affected by their decision. For example, a parent could say, "Suzie, how do you think the other children will feel if you give out your party invitations to your friends in front of the other children who aren't invited?"

Children may also need to have their feelings clarified regarding circumstances which have affected them.

So a loving relationship which is honest and open will provide opportunities for children and parents to discuss how life's events affect them.

5. Providing a JUST Home Environment

A home that encourages love and empathy will also encourage justice, which is an equal consideration for all family members. The Scriptures emphasize the importance of justice. In the Old Testament we read: "What does the Lord require of you? To act justly and to love mercy and to walk humbly with your God" (Mic. 6:8).

Children who are treated fairly are more likely to develop faster morally than when they experience constant injustice. In fact, as Christian educator Ted Ward notes: "Nothing has more influence on the development of moral judgment than participation in a just environment."[3]

What are ways that the home environment can be just? (Encourage group response. Ideas: respect for the feelings and opinions of every family member, being consistent in terms of rules or guidelines, drawing out the opinions of children in setting rules, and so on.)

Admittedly, a person's view of justice may be quite self-centered and related to rewards and punishments for themselves. But the more mature person is able to see justice in terms of other persons.

6. Provide an INTELLECTUALLY STIMULATING Home Environment

The child's growing mind is an important factor in the development of a sense of morality. Frequent dialogue with children about their opinions, feelings, and needs is critical for both intellectual and moral growth.

In discussing a concern with a child, a parent can ask: "What do you think about this?" "What are other ways we might do this?" "How might your friend feel about this?" It is important to encourage our children to stretch their thinking in learning to cope with life.

Books, magazines, records, school materials, and television programs can provide opportunities for discussion about important topics of concern. Creative activities such as drawing, painting, modeling with clay, cutting, or pasting also provide opportunities for interaction.

7. Conclusion

So, a home environment in which children are both loved and accepted, where they feel a sense of responsibility in helping the family function in a just manner, where they are encouraged to grow intellectually, provides the best setting for the development of an adequate system of values. And this environment can help a family be the family God wants it to be.

Sharing Together: Fishbowl/Roleplay Discussion (20-25 minutes)

Arrange the chairs in your room so that there is an inner circle of four chairs and an outer circle for all of the other chairs.

Ask for four volunteers, two to roleplay being parents, two to roleplay being adolescents. (Note: You may want to recruit these volunteers ahead of time.)

Introduce the activity by saying that the group will have opportunity to watch a "family" deal with a difficult issue—the children's choice of friends. (Option: Have the group identify another sensitive issue.)

Tell the four volunteers that they are to do the roleplay two times. The first time, the four people should be quite hostile and condemning of each other as they deal with the children's choice of friends.

After three or four minutes, ask the "family" to

do their discussing again, but this time seeking to share feelings, be open, draw each other out, and seek compromise.

Encourage the group to observe without reacting with laughter or talking. As the "family" does the roleplay the second time, ask the group to watch for differences between the two processes.

Next, guide the group in discussing what happened. First ask the "family" members to describe how they felt each time. Then ask group members to contrast the two experiences. Why is it difficult to be open and loving when resolving conflicts in the family? (Feelings get hurt, people begin raising their voices, egos get involved, and so on.)

Optional Activity

Encourage participants to reflect on what their own home environments are like, and to identify an area or two they would plan to change.

Distribute sheets of blank paper to everyone. Ask group members to write letters to themselves, in which they deal with the following areas (which you have written on chalkboard or newsprint):

When I think about our home environment, I feel good about . . .

I would like to work on improving . . .

After the letters have been written, they should be placed in envelopes and sealed. Ask everyone to print his or her name on the front of the envelope, and then collect all the envelopes. (You will distribute the letters at the conclusion of the last session of this course.)

Family Application (5-10 minutes)

Teaching the value of respect for the elderly.

Respect for the elderly is a value too commonly lacking in today's society, and Christian parents often wonder how they can foster an attitude among their children which values and sees that "Gray hair is a crown of splendor" (Prov. 16:31).

This session on enhancing the home environment is an ideal occasion to consider the development of this value, because it is in an environment of respect that respect is cultivated.

Have the class members suggest aspects of respect that may bear on this value's development, and list them on the chalkboard. The following are suggested examples:

· Respect for children's privacy, ideas, and time will elicit the same from them for others.

· Do you want your children to use "Mr." and "Mrs." when referring to other adults? Do you do the same when speaking of those significantly older than yourself?

· Do you berate grandparents so the children hear? Or do you build them up and honor them?

· Do you rise when an older person enters the room or offer him or her your seat?

Some of these practices or those suggested in class may not seem important to everyone, but parents should recognize that they will not get more respect (in the long run) than they are prepared to give. We will reap what we sow.

Wrap-Up (5 minutes)

We have been reminded in this session that the atmosphere in our home environments—those qualities which exemplify our relationships with other family members—has a subtle but lasting impact on all of the family members.

Ask a participant to conclude with prayer that God will give insight to discern how to strengthen what is already good in our families, and to change what needs to be changed.

Notes
[1]Virginia Satir, *Peoplemaking* (Palo Alto, Cal.: Science and Behavior Books, 1972), p. 197.
[2]Catherine M. Stonehouse, *Patterns in Moral Development* (Waco, Tex.: Word, Inc., 1980), pp. 50, 51.
[3]Ted Ward, *Values Begin at Home* (Wheaton, Ill.: Victor Books, 1979), p. 75.

SESSION 10 · MODELING CHRISTIAN VALUES

Objectives—To help people:

· REMINISCE about people who were influential examples to them during the growing up years.
· LIST characteristics of the positive Christian example.
· EVALUATE various styles of parental leadership.
· PRACTICE communication skills which enhance family relationships.

Advance Preparation

Have available:
1. TR-13 ("Styles of Family Leadership").
2. An overhead projector and screen.
3. Copies of RM-10 ("Communication in the Family")—one for each participant.
4. A chalkboard or newsprint.

Getting Started: Neighbor Judge (10-15 minutes)

Welcome everyone to your group. Thank God for all of the opportunities for sharing and learning which have already taken place, and for what is yet to come.

Divide the group into pairs. Ask participants to share with each other regarding these questions: *Think back to your childhood and adolescent years. Who were people who significantly influenced you? What was it about them that so impressed you?*

After people have had a few minutes to share, gather back in the large group. Ask participants to share qualities of these influential people. Develop a composite list on chalkboard or newsprint.

Exploring Together: Being an Example (15-20 minutes)

1. Introduction
Refer to your composite list. Note that the people who most heavily influenced us were probably those with whom there were strong emotional bonds. We have learned from others not only through receiving information from them, but we have "caught" important teachings regarding our faith and values through observing people we have admired, and we sought to imitate them.

2. Being an Example
As we learned in our last session, the environment of the home greatly influences the moral development of our children. Another significant way that our children develop Christian values is through observing and identifying with us, their parents.

Researcher Norman J. Bull went so far as to say, "The nature of a child's morality will depend upon those around him—upon, that is, the identifications he makes."[1]

Albert Bandura has defined identification as "a process in which a person patterns his thoughts, feelings, or actions after another person who serves as a model."[2]

Many researchers maintain that observing the behaviors of others has a powerful impact upon our behavior, as well as upon the development of our attitudes and values.

Jesus certainly used this modeling style of teaching in His earthly ministry. Rather than give all of His energies to speaking to large crowds, Jesus concentrated great amounts of time to be with His disciples—to share life together, to train them in His teachings, to prepare them to live as believers after He returned to Heaven.

And Jesus' approach worked. The time the disciples spent observing and learning from Jesus made a significant impact on their ministry in the early church. And much of their own development took place as they listened, watched, evaluated, and interacted with Jesus.

For children and adolescents, parents serve as models for most behaviors and values. Christian educator Larry Richards maintains that "one learns his likeness through seeing that likeness lived in others with whom he identifies."[3]

In fact, Jesus said, "Everyone who is fully trained will be like his teacher" (Lk. 6:40).

When it comes specifically to the teaching of values, then, we see that values can be taught, explained, and expressed in words. (In fact, that is the subject of our next session.) But our values will more likely be understood and accepted if we are modeling them in the context of a loving relationship. Through living our faith and values, we show our children how to live their own faith.

What are ways we can be examples to our children? (Allow a few moments for group sharing. Ideas: the ways we relate to other adults, how we handle parent-child conflicts, what we have done with past hurts, telling the truth, and so on.)

3. Decision Making and Leadership
A significant part of being an example and encouraging the development of healthy values is shown in our style of leadership in the home. (Refer to TR-13, "Styles of Family Leadership," as you review this material.)

There are three basic styles of family leadership: authoritarian, permissive, and democratic. Again, we need to acknowledge that many of us would find ourselves using two or more styles, depending on what seemed appropriate. But we might tend to use one style more than the others.

An authoritarian home is one in which there is little discussion, in which family decisions are handed down from parents to children without opportunity for interaction. An authoritarian home does not take into account the growing need of children to learn to participate in family decisions and to make decisions which will help them become mature, independent, empathic, moral persons. Communication and closeness in authoritarian homes frequently do not exist.

A permissive home, on the other hand, does not foster closeness or open communication either. In a permissive home, children often seem to be raising themselves. Parents are frequently preoccupied with their own interests and do not provide any kind of leadership for the family. Children often rebel because of a lack of bonding within the family. They may seek to draw attention to themselves through whatever means are at their disposal.

A democratic home is one in which there is frequent discussion regarding decisions which affect family members. Kohlberg sees great importance in mutual sharing in appropriate family decisions and giving increasing responsibility to the child. Such an environment gives children a feeling of participation and confidence, and encourages them to voice feelings and opinions within the family.

The home in which there is ongoing interchange, where children are encouraged to express their feelings constructively and their opinions freely, will make a lasting contribution to the child's development of a meaningful value system.

Parents can profit from being open in stating their own beliefs, but not demanding total agreement from everyone on every issue. Parents should also refrain from expressing horror or disgust at what their children say. Too strong a negative reaction may cause a child to withdraw from openly expressing feelings or ideas in the future. If the opinion of the child should be corrected, this can be done in a respectful, instructive way. If the way the child spoke was sassy or inappropriate, that, too, should be addressed.

We need to draw an important distinction at this point between being authoritarian and being authoritative. In striving to be democratic, parents need not feel they are abdicating the authority God has given them to be leaders in their families. There are certainly times when we need to make decisions for our families, to be firm but loving in our guidance. To be democratic in family leadership may not mean "one person, one vote." The nature of the decision, the age and understanding of the child,

and who will be affected most must be considered. And as parents we must accept the final responsibility for all decisions. But this does not mean that we have to assume a domineering, dictatorial style of leadership which ignores or rejects the feelings and opinions of other family members. Listening and considering the perspectives of everyone is the key to the democratic family.

What are examples of times when parents may have to make decisions, no matter what the opinions of the children may be? (Take a few moments to share ideas. Suggestions: matters which are of concern only to a married couple, such as their intimacy; times when compromise seems impossible; etc.)

What are examples of decisions where equal votes may be granted to all? (Where to go on a family outing; what to have for some meals; how the family room might be decorated; etc.)

What are examples of the more common decisions which might fall between these two extremes, where the opinions and feelings of the children are heard and considered by the parents as they make the decision? (Job choice, where to live, what to watch on TV, etc.)

The important point we want to make is that children can be consulted on many decisions a family faces. And when they are involved in the decision-making process, their self-esteem is enhanced. As children feel respected, they will tend to be more respectful regarding the needs and feelings of others.

4. Conclusion

We need to ask God frequently to help us be the kinds of examples He wants us to be. Consistency and Christlikeness are especially important.

But at the same time, we need to recognize that our children's values are influenced by other people as well. We do not need to feel that our example is the only determining influence. As adults, we are also in a process of growth. We acknowledge that at times we fail, that we are not capable of being God's best in every situation.

haring Together:
ommunication Exercise
0-25 minutes)

Distribute copies of the "Communication in the Family" handout (RM-10).

Divide the class into small groups of three or four. Encourage group members to work together to decide how each situation described on this work sheet could be handled with an authoritarian response, a permissive response, and a democratic response. (Option: You may want to assign two or three of the situations to each group if your time is limited.)

If the directions seem unclear, do the first situation in the large group. Ask: *When the table needs to be set for a meal, what would be an authoritarian response?* (Suggestion if group is slow to respond: "I don't care how you feel; set the table!")

What would be a permissive response? (Suggestion: "Eat when you want. I'm busy right now.")

What about a democratic response? (Suggestion: "It's important that we all do our part in keeping this family going. Let's agree on who will set the table each day.")

After small groups have completed the activity, gather back in the large group and share responses.

amily Application (5-10
inutes)

Teaching the value of family unity.

"I pray [that] . . . they be brought to complete unity" (Jn. 17:20, 23). This plea by Jesus for the unity of the Church must begin to be answered in our homes with true family unity. Christ said the validation of His whole mission would rest on this value: ". . . to let the world know that you sent me and have loved them even as you have loved me" (vs. 23). That gives it a pretty high priority.

How can we instill this value in our children? How can real family unity become important to them? First of all by making it important to us! In this session we spent considerable time on styles of family leadership, emphasizing the importance of considering the perspectives of the children in family decision making. If we want them to care about family unity, then we need to care about it. We need to be concerned to not run roughshod over them. We may frequently not be able to do just what they want, but that should matter to us. And, when appropriate, attempts should be made to explain, to bring understanding, and to arrive at agreement.

Children raised in such an environment will know that keeping the family together (not just physically) is important. They will value that unity and hesitate to break it themselves.

Such unity in the family does not rule out diversity, for there is to be much diversity in the Church, too. The Bible encourages diverse gifts and functions and exemplifies ways differing opinions and approaches can coexist in unity.

Children from authoritarian or permissive families will tend to think there is no value in family unity. In authoritarian families, the appearance of unity may exist as long as the parents have the power to impose their unilateral will. But rebellion will come. In permissive families, even the appearance of unity is absent as everyone does his or her own thing.

We can pray, as Jesus prayed, for true unity. And if preserving it matters to us, it will matter to our children.

Wrap-Up (5 minutes)

As we have seen, modeling Christian values is one of the most powerful ways we teach our children. Who we are and how we act greatly influences the values our children develop.

Thank God for the great privilege of being parents and for the growth you experience because of this great challenge.

Ask people to bring any books or other resources for family activities to the next session to share.

Notes

[1]Norman J. Bull, *Moral Education* (London: Routledge and Kegan, 1969), p. 15.

[2]Albert Bandura, "Social-Learning Theory of Identificatory Processes," in *Handbook of Socialization Theory and Research* (Chicago: Rand McNally College Publishing Company, 1969), p. 214.

[3]Lawrence O. Richards, *A Theology of Christian Education* (Grand Rapids, Mich.: Zondervan Publishing House, 1975), p. 84.

SESSION 11 · TEACHING CHRISTIAN VALUES

Objectives—To help people:

· LIST barriers to quality time.
· DESCRIBE how these barriers can be overcome.
· DIFFERENTIATE between informal and formal teaching in the family.
· PLAN ways to teach values (both informally and formally) at home.

Advance Preparation

Have available:
1. TR-14 ("Teaching in the Family").
2. An overhead projector and screen.
3. Blank paper and pencils for the Getting Together activity.
4. Copies of RM-11 ("Family Activities That Build Values"), one for each participant.
5. Family activity resources (see bibliography for ideas) set out on a large table.
6. A chalkboard or newsprint.

Getting Started: Brainstorming (10-15 minutes)

Thank God for the learning which has taken place; ask for God's continuing help in implementing these ideas in our families.

Divide into groups of three or four. Ask the groups to make a list of barriers which keep families from having quality time together. Ask groups to each appoint a recorder for making the list.

After several minutes, reassemble in the large group. Have the recorders share their lists. Use a chalkboard or newsprint to develop a composite list of these barriers.

After the list has been compiled, ask participants which barriers seem to be particularly difficult to overcome.

Exploring Together: Teaching in the Family (15-20 minutes)

1. Introduction

A significant factor in helping our children develop Christian values is having quality time together—time in which family members can enjoy each other and learn together. (Refer back to the list of barriers.) Building time for our families into our busy schedules is an enormous task for all of us.

But such efforts will be well worth it in the long run. We will work together in this session to find ways to spend quality time together, so that our teaching of values can be enhanced.

2. Kinds of Learning

There are two important kinds of learning which we can do in our families: formal and informal learning. (Refer to TR-14, "Teaching in the Family.")

Formal learning is like that done in the classroom. For the family, there may be a structured discussion or activity, or enjoying a story together. Such learning often takes place in what some families call "Family Times"—special time set aside each week for such learning experiences.

Informal learning is like that done on a science class field trip. It is learning by doing, discovering, and testing. For the family, informal learning takes place constantly—while eating, doing dishes, doing chores, going on hikes, playing games, relating to relatives, and so on.

The Scriptures talk about both kinds of learning. In Proverbs, we read of formal instruction which parents are expected to do with their children. (Read Prov. 1:8; 4:1-4.)

We also find that Scripture encourages the informal kinds of learning which takes place more spontaneously throughout the day. (Refer to Deut. 6:4-9 as an example.)

Both kinds of learning are appropriate in the right setting. But just as our behaviors may be more influential than our words, so informal learning may, in the long run, have as much impact upon our children as more structured experiences.

Let's talk in a little more detail about each kind of learning.

3. Informal Learning in the Family

What are situations in which informal learning takes place in the family? (Encourage participants to respond. Ideas: A family event, such as the birth of a child, death of a relative, loss of a job, moving, conflict with a friend, when riding in the car, hiking, playing a game, and so on.)

As we learned in the session on enhancing the home environment, there is great value in using communication skills in these informal situations. Asking questions and drawing the children into dialogue regarding their ideas and feelings are examples of enhancing informal learning.

Remember that we can learn from children as well. (See Mt. 19:13-15.) *We can learn from their responses to informal situations just as they can learn from us. A simple, childlike faith is helpful for all of us to observe.*

Even though informal learning may often be

rather spontaneous, it is important to include informal times in our busy calendars so that such learning can take place.

4. More Structured Learning in the Family

Many families find that they profit from having a Family Time regularly, a time when all family members agree to be at home and spend time together. Families may fix a special meal together and then enjoy favorite family activities. There may be a time for study and discussion of a Bible story or theme. (If possible, share an example or two of what you have done in your own family. Encourage a few other participants to share what has worked for them.)

Timing is often a key concern, because of busy or conflicting schedules. For some families, an evening is best. For others, a block of time on a Saturday or Sunday works well.

In such learning, leadership can be shared among whoever is involved. Children and young people will grow in their self-worth and confidence as they have opportunity to share in the leadership of these family times.

5. Conclusion

Refer again to the list of barriers. Spend a few moments getting group thoughts about how to overcome these barriers.

Again, having quality time together as families is an important value. And if family togetherness is really a value, we will find a way to have such time together. We may find it hard work to build in such time. But if we don't make the effort, those times will rarely happen spontaneously.

As many families can testify, these Family Times can be some of the most significant experiences we can have together as families.

Sharing Together: Sharing and Planning (20-25 minutes)

Divide the class into smaller groups of four or five. Encourage participants to share their thoughts and feelings about informal and more structured learning in the family.

Have participants review the available resources you have collected (from your own library, your church library, other class members, and so on).

Guide people to look for specific ideas and activities they would like to try at home in the next week or two.

Be sure everyone has a copy of the "Family Activities That Build Values" handout (RM-11) for additional ideas.

Ask that everyone share their plans in the small groups and that people pray for each other about implementing these plans.

Distribute slips of paper to the small groups. Ask each group to think of one or more specific questions regarding moral development and values which they would like discussed in the next session. The questions could begin with: "What do I do when . . .?" Be sure that you have at least five to ten questions available for the next session.

Family Application (5-10 minutes)

Teaching the value of courage.

"Be strong and courageous . . . Do not be afraid; do not be discouraged" (Deut. 31:7, 8). Courage, like many other character qualities, can be devalued in our society and be replaced by things like appearance, wealth, and conformity.

In this session we have noted the difference between formal and informal learning situations. One of the most enjoyable formal ways to cultivate Christian values in our children is through reading Christian biographies. Some families make it a practice to always have a family book which they read from each evening after the meal for 20 minutes or so. The stories of Christian martyrs, the great missionary heroes, and many contemporary Christians offer powerful examples of courage (as well as other important character qualities). Such qualities are always necessary for victorious Christian living, and if the person's life was worthy of recording, those qualities will be evident. Brief discussions at significant points in the story can draw attention to courage or other qualities in a powerful way, and the whole family can enjoy it.

Wrap-Up (5 minutes)

Providing quality time for our families is one of the most perplexing issues we need to deal with in our busy lives. But, as we have said before, the ways we invest our time is a significant indicator of what is important to us and is a powerful example to our children of what our values really are.

Conclude with prayer. Ask that several persons pray brief prayers, thanking God for His loving care and for the courage He can give us to live with the right priorities.

SESSION 12 · WHAT DO I DO WHEN . . . ?

Objectives—To help people:

· RELATE Christian values to specific family conflicts.
· DESCRIBE an effective approach to working through differences.
· SHARE areas of personal and family needs.
· PRAY for God's help in relieving anxieties about family concerns and strengthening family relationships.

Advance Preparation

Have available:
1. The following words printed on chalkboard or newsprint:

> When I think my ___-year-old child is making a wrong decision about _____ , I should . . .
> ___convince the child to change.
> ___have someone else talk to the child.
> ___punish the child.
> ___let the child go ahead, even if the child may fail or do wrong.
> ___discuss the consequences with the child.
> ___pray with the child.
> ___call the pastor.
> ___get angry.

2. A shoe box or other small box labeled "Question Box," containing the questions from the previous session.
3. TR-15 ("Problems, Problems, Problems").
4. An overhead projector and screen.
5. Copies of RM-12 ("Guidelines for Working Through Differences") and RM-13 ("Case Studies")—one copy of each handout for each participant.
6. A chalkboard or newsprint.
7. Recruit several persons for a panel discussion if Option I for the Exploring Together time is used.

Getting Started: Multiple Choice Discussion (10-15 minutes)

As you begin this session, ask God to give participants special insight as they seek to apply all of the Christian principles they have been learning to specific family situations.

Acknowledge that many times decision making in the family, especially regarding values, is quite complex. Our feelings can affect our attitudes and beliefs.

Refer to the chalkboard or newsprint and the options under the heading, "When I think my ___-year-old child is making a wrong decision about _____ , I should . . ." (See "Advance Preparation.") Ask the class to supply an age and a situation to consider. (An 11-year-old wanting to smoke would obviously be treated differently than a 15-year-old choosing to take a drama class instead of home economics.) Also, ask the participants whether they have any other alternative responses to add to the list.

Have persons choose responses they would most agree with. Poll the group and jot down the number of persons choosing each response. Divide into groups according to the responses people have selected. Keep groups smaller than six persons. If any response received a greater number, divide it into two or more groups for those alternatives.

Have people list the assumptions which underlie their choice. How will this alternative enhance the development of values? Why are the other choices not as preferable?

Option: Assign one of the alternative responses to each group and have them complete the same process.

Then share small group ideas in the large group.

Exploring Together: Working Through Differences (15-2_ minutes_

1. Introduction

Briefly review the questions from the Question Box which group members had written in the previous session. Ask if there are any other concerns regarding values with which the group should deal.

2. Consideration of Group Concerns

Explain to the group that there will be more group involvement in this session than in previous ones, as together you seek to apply all that has been learned to specific family concerns. There are at least two format options you could follow:

OPTION I: PANEL DISCUSSION

Have a few volunteers (or those who agreed ahead of time) be a panel to discuss as many questions as time permits. Give one or more of the questions to each panel member. After they give brief, initial responses, encourage interaction among the other panel members. Be sure to include participation from the rest of the class as well.

OPTION II: SMALL GROUP DISCUSSION

Assign one or more questions to each of several small groups. Guide the small groups to explore each question assigned to them. Then have a time of sharing responses back in the large group.

Whichever approach you use, be sure that participants do the following:

· Identify Scriptural principles and guidelines which are particularly appropriate to each situation.

· Identify two or more alternative responses to each dilemma.

· Identify any practical considerations which would influence the choice among various options.

3. Working Through Differences in the Family

Decision making in the family is particularly challenging when some issues arouse great difference of feeling. Sometimes there can be a feeling that communication is cut off, that people don't really care about the feelings or ideas of the others, only that their way win out. (Refer to TR-15, "Problems, Problems, Problems.")

Families can benefit from learning a process for working through some of their differences—a process which seeks to help each family member identify what is being felt and to find areas of compromise wherever possible. (Read and discuss the "Guidelines for Working Through Differences" handout, RM-12, with participants.)

What are situations when this process would be particularly helpful? (Guide group members to brainstorm a list of possibilities: a possible move to a new area; choice of friends, and so on.)

What might make such a process difficult? (Again, share ideas. Suggestion: When feelings are very strong on both sides and neither can talk clearly to each other.)

Sharing Together: Case Studies (20-25 minutes)

Distribute copies of the "Case Studies" handout (RM-13). Note that there are three situations: one involving preschool-age children, one focusing upon elementary-age children, and one involving adolescent young people.

Have people divide into small groups according to the age level of their children, or the case study of most interest to them.

If there are more than eight people in any one group, divide into smaller groups of no more than six to eight each.

Encourage people to use the "Guidelines" handout (RM-12) as they discuss the situations described in the case studies.

As time permits, have the groups gather again in the large group to hear the responses of each group.

Family application (5-10 minutes)

Teaching the value of peaceful resolutions.

"Wisdom is better than weapons of war" (Eccl. 9:18). It may be possible to get your way by strength, if you are mighty enough. But if we teach our children that this approach is valid, they are sure to meet someone who is stronger than they are and may pay painfully in their defeat.

In this session we have been looking at ways to work through differences in values within the family. Working out conflicts in a peaceful way is in itself an important value.

The value of peaceful resolution to differences may seem like a common expectation in our society, and yet a closer look may reveal that much of that assumption is just diplomatic talk. The bottom line in many international disputes is power, and that is what dictates many social and family relationships as well. The Bible suggests a better way all around, and we can begin developing an appreciation for the wisdom of truly peaceful resolution within our families if we as parents practice the skill of compromise (in nonethical matters) and practice the attitude of love which puts the welfare of the other person before our own.

When efforts are being made to work out differences within the family, the teaching of values is enhanced when those values are identified as the operating principles. For instance, the value of peaceful resolution is underlined by explicitly stating, "Now, we want to work this out peacefully in a way that everyone can accept." If there is integrity in the discussion which follows, the value will be greatly reinforced and will in time become the objective the children work toward and cherish.

Wrap-Up (5 minutes)

There are often many ways to approach the same problem and families may handle such problems in several ways. What is important is that our faith be central to any decision making and, if at all possible, the family relationship be preserved. Close with conversational prayer.

Objectives—To help people:

· SHARE specific ways the course has been helpful personally and for their families.
· PARTICIPATE in a worship experience.
· RESOLVE ways to strengthen family relationships, especially as related to values.
· COMMIT the needs and concerns of their families to God.

Advance Preparation

Have available:
1. TR-16 ("Celebration Songs").
2. An overhead projector and screen.
3. Copies of RM-14 ("Looking Back, Looking Forward"), RM-15 ("Evaluation of Learning Experience"), and RM-16 ("Celebration Responsive Reading"), one copy of each handout for each participant.
4. A sheet of paper on which you have lettered at top: "PRAYER PARTNER SIGN UP." Post near exit of your room.
5. The letters written in Session 9 (if that activity was used).

Getting Started: Sentence Completion Exercise (10-15 minutes)

Welcome everyone to this last session of the course. Express thanks to God for all that has been experienced and learned. Pray for the ability to implement our faith while facing complex moral dilemmas as well as the more simple decisions of life.

Distribute copies of the "Looking Back, Looking Forward" (RM-14) handout.

Divide into groups of three or four. Have people complete the exercise individually, then share their responses in the small groups.

Exploring Together: Looking Back, Looking Forward (15-20 minutes)

1. Review of Key Concepts

As time permits, briefly review the key concepts which have been considered in this course. Use any of the transparencies which would strengthen this review.
· Values develop through a series of stages and can be quite different for young children, in comparison to adults.

· The family is important for healthy development—physically, emotionally, socially, morally, and spiritually.
· Our faith in Jesus Christ is at the core of our lives, including dealing with moral dilemmas.
· We also have the use of the Scriptures, traditions, our reason, consciences, and the Holy Spirit.
· As parents, we can more effectively facilitate the development of values in our children as we enhance our home environments, so that they are loving, empathetic, just, and intellectually stimulating.
· Perhaps our greatest influence on the moral development of our children takes place through the modeling we do of Christian values—in our attitudes and actions, as well as words.
· We can enhance the development of values for our children informally through unstructured family activities, as well as through more structured Family Times.

2. Personal Sharing

Be prepared to share for a few minutes regarding what this learning experience has meant to you personally. Jot down your thoughts in response to the following questions, and be prepared to share your answers to two or three of them:

· What personal growth has resulted because of this learning experience?

· What have you appreciated about the participants?

· What have you learned from the participants, as well as from the curriculum and the Scriptures?

· What pertinent questions have been raised for your consideration?

· What questions have been answered?

· How have your family relationships been strengthened because of what you have learned?

· *What do you plan to do with what you have learned?*

· *What areas of concern need further exploration?*

Other thoughts for your sharing:

3. Group Sharing

As time permits, ask group members to share what the course has meant to them. What has been most helpful? Encourage brief responses so that several people can share.

4. Course Evaluation

Distribute copies of the "Evaluation of Learning Experience" handout (RM-15). Take a few moments for participants to complete the evaluation form. Then collect the forms for your review.

5. Looking Ahead

Share briefly regarding any future plans for your group. Will there be any other learning experiences related to parenting or family life? As time permits, encourage participants to suggest what other kinds of learning experiences would be helpful to them. (Be sure that this information is shared with those planning adult education experiences in your church.)

Indicate that one of the most helpful parts of these learning experiences can be the development of a support system among people with similar interests and needs. An effective way churches have found for developing such a support system is through organizing a "prayer partner" network. Explain that two people agree to pray for each other daily, and to keep in touch by phone or in person at least once a week for two months. Conversations should center on sharing needs, prayer requests, reports of progress, and so on. At the end of the two months, the prayer partners decide whether or not they wish to continue.

Ask those who are interested to sign up on a sheet of paper which you have posted near the exit.

(Be sure that you or someone else assumes responsibility for coordinating this effort. Someone will need to pair off the partners and contact everyone.)

Family Application (5-10 minutes)

Teaching the value of God's creation.

Explain that before dismissing you'd like to offer one final sample value with a suggestion for cultivating it in the family.

"God saw all that he had made, and it was very good" (Gen. 1: 31). God didn't make any mistakes when He created you or your children. Each individual is so valuable that God sent His Son to redeem us. There could be no greater value established.

You may have noticed that almost every Family Application example returns to the practice of the family *as the primary tool for transmitting that value. That's by design. God said that His creation was good, and His declaring that value should be enough for us to accept it. But the real clincher is in what He* did *to express that value—the sacrifice of His Son to redeem His creation.*

And so it is what we do *in our families that will develop values, even more than what we say. Do you want to teach the value of God's creation to your children? Just take them out in it, and give them many opportunities to enjoy God's creatures and natural wonders. Show them by your respect and good stewardship of nature and its resources that it means a lot to you. It's what you do, as it is what God has done, which is most important.*

Sharing Together: Celebration (20-25 minutes)

The format for this final Sharing Together time is a variation from previous sessions. The group will have a worship and sharing time which will involve both large- and small-group experiences.

Distribute copies of the "Celebration Responsive Reading" handout (RM-16) as you begin.

Song. "Love, Love." Refer to TR-16, "Celebration Songs" (cover bottom half of transparency). If this song is new to most people, sing through it at least twice, so that everyone can sing the song with confidence. Option: In a larger group, the song is particularly beautiful when sung in a round.

Responsive reading. As an expression of the group's thoughts and feelings regarding this learning experience, as well as of your faith, use

the "Celebration Responsive Reading." Be sure that everyone knows the sections they will be reading (left and right sides of the room, men or women, etc.).

Affirmation, sharing, and prayer. Divide into groups of three. Encourage the people in the groups to spend a few minutes affirming each other—identifying what they especially appreciate about the other person. Share any personal needs related to family and values. Encourage groups to pray together.

When the groups have completed this process, gather together back in the large group.

Wrap-U

Refer again to TR-16, "Celebration Songs." If the "Benediction" song is new to your group, be sure to sing it at least once to learn it and another time when people can sing with more confidence. Note that the song is sung in unison to the tune of "Edelweiss," from *The Sound of Music*. If this tune is unfamiliar, choose another song that your group can sing, such as, "God Is So Good."

Distribute letters written in Session 9 (if you did that activity). Close with a prayer.

Be available at the conclusion to answer questions or discuss concerns with group members.

TEACHING CHRISTIAN VALUES IN THE FAMILY
A Learning Experience for Parents

Sponsoring organization   Instructor

SCHEDULE:
(Dates)

COURSE SCHEDULE

_____ 1. **Introductory Session**
Get-acquainted; foundations

_____ 2. **How Do Values Develop?**
Overview of values development from early childhood to adulthood

_____ 3. **What Is the Role of the Family?**
Importance of the family for moral development

_____ 4. **What Do I Value?**
Identifying and evaluating my own values

_____ 5. **What's Our Guide?**
Scriptures; tradition and church teachings; reason; conscience; the Holy Spirit and personal decisions

_____ 6. **Jesus and Values**
The teachings and example of Jesus regarding values

_____ 7. **What Are Essential Christian Values?**
Identifying important Christian values

_____ 8. **What Do I Do When Values Conflict?**
Primary and secondary values

_____ 9. **Enhancing the Home Environment**
The importance of quality relationships

_____ 10. **Modeling Christian Values**
The importance of being an example

_____ 11. **Teaching Christian Values**
Informal and formal teaching in the home

_____ 12. **What Do I Do When . . . ?**
Dealing with difficult moral dilemmas in the family

_____ 13. **Finally . . .**
Evaluation; looking ahead; concluding celebration

TEACHING CHRISTIAN VALUES IN THE FAMILY
A Learning Experience for Parents

Sponsoring organization _____

Instructor _____

COURSE SCHEDULE

SCHEDULE:
(Dates)

_____ 1. **Introductory Session**
Get-acquainted; foundations

_____ 2. **How Do Values Develop?**
Overview of values development from early childhood to adulthood

_____ 3. **What Is the Role of the Family?**
Importance of the family for moral development

_____ 4. **What Do I Value?**
Identifying and evaluating my own values

_____ 5. **What's Our Guide?**
Scriptures; tradition and church teachings; reason; conscience;
the Holy Spirit and personal decisions

_____ 6. **Jesus and Values**
The teachings and example of Jesus regarding values

_____ 7. **What Are Essential Christian Values?**
Identifying important Christian values

_____ 8. **What Do I Do When Values Conflict?**
Primary and secondary values

_____ 9. **Enhancing the Home Environment**
The importance of quality relationships

_____ 10. **Modeling Christian Values**
The importance of being an example

_____ 11. **Teaching Christian Values**
Informal and formal teaching in the home

_____ 12. **What Do I Do When . . . ?**
Dealing with difficult moral dilemmas in the family

_____ 13. **Finally . . .**
Evaluation; looking ahead; concluding celebration

TEACHING CHRISTIAN VALUES IN THE FAMILY
A Learning Experience for Parents

Sponsoring organization _____ Instructor _____

SCHEDULE:
(Date)

COURSE SCHEDULE

1. Introductory Session
   Get acquainted; introductions

2. How Do Values Develop?
   Overview of values development from early childhood to adulthood

3. What Is the Role of the Family?
   Importance of the family as a value-forming group

4. What Do I Value?
   Identifying and evaluating our own values

5. What's Our Guide?
   Scripture, tradition, and church teachings; forming conscience; the Holy Spirit and personal decisions

6. Icons and Values
   The teachings and examples of other teaching bodies

7. What Are Essential Christian Values?
   Identifying important Christian values

8. What Are Our Secondary Values?
   Primary and secondary values

9. Enhancing the Value Statement
   The importance of quality relationships

10. Modeling Christian Values
    The importance of living by example

11. Teaching Christian Values
    Informal and formal instruction in the home

12. When Do I Do What . . . ?
    Dealing with distinct value differences in the family

13. Finally . . .
    Evaluation; looking ahead; completing certification

A FAMILY STORY

Steve, the father, has his own business and often has to work evenings or weekends, when it is convenient for his clients. Steve has recently felt tired and strained. He has ambivalent feelings toward his wife's part-time job: he appreciates the second income, but he also feels guilty about the amount of time he has to be away from home and wishes his wife were home to cover responsibilities with the children that he is unable or too tired to carry out.

..........(cut)..

Janet, the mother, has recently gone to work part-time in a clothing shop. It was a big adjustment at first in the family schedule. Now Janet enjoys her job, and she has begun to acquire a finer taste in clothing. She does not arrive home until an hour and a half after the children are out of school. Then Janet is sometimes upset because Ben has not done his chores. She has also become more critical of the sloppy way her daughter dresses and has been nagging her recently to go shopping for skirts and sweaters instead of the jeans and T-shirts Patty prefers.

.... (cut) ....

Patty, the daughter, has seemed fairly indifferent to the new family schedule. In fact, at 14, she likes the new feeling of independence and not having to get right home after school. She's been getting in more fights with her mother over clothes and has been resisting her mother's efforts to get her to "dress up." She feels her mother doesn't understand how important it is to wear what the other kids do, from colored laces in gym shoes to certain kinds of jeans. Patty occasionally baby-sits to earn spending money, but it's often not enough to buy the kinds of clothes she likes to wear. She's sure her mother won't fork over money without dictating what she has to buy. Dad would probably give her the money—but he's often not around and seems worried about money lately.

..........(cut)..

Ben, the brother, likes to hang around home building stuff in the basement or playing with friends in the backyard. He dislikes the new family schedule, especially because often not even Patty is home when he gets home from school. Ben doesn't like having to do more chores now that Mom works and often conveniently "forgets" or puts everything off until the last minute. He was the one who took the phone call from the police.

.... (cut) ....

EVALUATION QUESTIONS

After roleplaying how the Jones family deals with this situation from the characters' viewpoints, discuss the following:

1. Where did the "blame" for the situation tend to fall, according to each family member?

2. What feelings about situations or family members **other** than Patty and the shoplifting came out in this interaction?

3. What did the family members learn about each other in this interaction?

4. What response to Patty did each one have? What was Patty's own response?

5. What values were expressed by individual family members? Did these differ from each other? How were they the same?

6. How did hearing from each other about what each valued help them work toward a solution to this situation?

7. Was the family able to clarify which values they wanted to be in unity about?

A FAMILY STORY

Steve, the father, has his own business and often has to work evenings or weekends when it is convenient for his clients. Steve has recently felt tired and strained. He has ambivalent feelings toward his wife's part-time job: he appreciates the second income, but he also feels guilty about the amount of time he has to be away from home and wishes his wife were home to cover responsibilities with the children that he is unable to or too tired to carry out.

.... (cut).

Janet, the mother, has recently gone to work part-time in a clothing shop. It was a big adjustment at first in the family schedule. Now Janet enjoys her job, and she has begun to acquire a finer taste in clothing. She does not arrive home until an hour and a half after the children are out of school. Then Janet is sometimes upset because Ben has not done his chores. She has also become more critical of the sloppy way her daughter dresses and has been nagging her recently to go shopping for skirts and sweaters instead of the jeans and T-shirts Patty prefers.

.... (cut) .....

Patty, the daughter, has seemed fairly indifferent to the new family schedule. In fact, at 14, she likes the new feeling of independence and not having to get right home after school. She's been getting in more fights with her mother over clothes and has been resisting her mother's efforts to get her to "dress up." She feels her mother doesn't understand how important it is to wear what the other kids do, from colored laces in gym shoes to certain kinds of jeans. Patty occasionally baby-sits to earn spending money, but it's often not enough to buy the kinds of clothes she likes to wear. She's sure her mother won't fork over money without dictating what she has to buy. Dad would probably give her the money—but he's often not around and seems worried about money lately.

.... (cut) .....

Ben, the brother, likes to hang around home building stuff in the basement or playing with friends in the backyard. He dislikes the new family schedule, especially because often not even Patty is home when he gets home from school. Ben doesn't like having to do more chores now that Mom works and often conveniently "forgets" or puts everything off until the last minute. He was the one who took the phone call from the police.

.... (cut) .....

EVALUATION QUESTIONS

After roleplaying how the Jones family deals with this situation from the characters' viewpoints, discuss the following:

1. Where did the "blame" for the situation tend to fall, according to each family member?

2. What feelings about situations or family members other than Patty and the shoplifting came out in this interaction?

3. What did the family members learn about each other in this interaction?

4. What response to Patty did each one have? What was Patty's own response?

5. What values were expressed by individual family members? Did these differ from each other? How were they the same?

6. How did hearing from each other about what each valued help them work toward a solution to this situation?

7. Was the family able to clarify which values they wanted to be in unity about?

A FAMILY STORY

Steve, the father, has his own business and often has to work evenings or weekends, when it is convenient for his clients. Steve has recently felt tired and strained. He has ambivalent feelings toward his wife's part-time job; he appreciates the second income, but he also feels guilty about the amount of time he has to be away from home and wishes his wife were home to share responsibilities with the children that he is unable or too tired to carry out.

(dit) ....

Janet, the mother, has recently given up work part-time in a clothing store. It was a big adjustment to live in the family situation, now Janet accept her job, and she has begun to occupy a fairer share in shopping. She does not relax her time until an hour or a bit after the children are out of school. Then Janet is something upset because Ben has not done his chores. She has also been resisting her mother's attempts to get her to "dress up." She feels uncomfortable in some expensive clothing, sure about whether she wants to know what the other kids do, from between times in some places to certain kinds of jeans. Betty consistently baby-sits to earn spending money, but it's often not enough to buy the kinds of clothes she likes to wear. She's sure her mother won't fork over money without dictating what she has to buy. Dad would probably give her the money—but he's often tired, stressed, and seems worried about money lately.

Betty, the daughter, has earned babysitting money. She has begun to enjoy the new feeling of independence and not having to get right home after school. She's been getting in more fights with her brother over clothes, and has been resisting her mother's attempts to get her to "dress up." She feels uncomfortable...

(dit) ....

Ben, the brother, likes to hang around home twisting stuff in the basement or playing with friends in the backyard. He dislikes the new chore schedule in general because often not with Betty is home when he gets home from school. He resents the tendency to do more chores now that Mom works and often complains. He'll argue over everything until the last minute. He has the answer that the gripes outdoes the peace.

.... (dit) ....

EVALUATION QUESTIONS

After studying how the Jones family deals with this situation from any character viewpoint, discuss the following:

1. Where did the "blame" for this situation seem to fall, according to each family member?

2. What feelings about situations or family members about Ben, Betty and the shoplifting came out in this interaction?

3. What did the family members learn about each other in this interaction?

4. What decisions really did each one make? What was his real response?

5. What values were expressed by individual family members, and how close they may each other, and were they the same?

6. How did Family Story come either about what each wanted help them work toward a solution in this situation?

7. Was the family able to clarify which values they wanted to be in unity about?

COAT OF ARMS

Make a coat of arms for yourself by drawing pictures of the following:

1. What occupies most of your time during the day?
2. What do you like to do when you are alone?
3. What do you like to do when you are with your family at home?
4. What do you like to do with your family when you are away from home?
5. What is your least favorite activity or chore?
6. What is something you have always wanted to do but have not done as yet?

1.   2.

3.   4.

5.   6.

COAT OF ARMS

Make a coat of arms for yourself by drawing pictures of the following:

1. What occupies most of your time during the day?
2. What do you like to do when you are alone?
3. What do you like to do when you are with your family at home?
4. What do you like to do with your family when you are away from home?
5. What is your least favorite activity or chore?
6. What is something you have always wanted to do but have not done as yet?

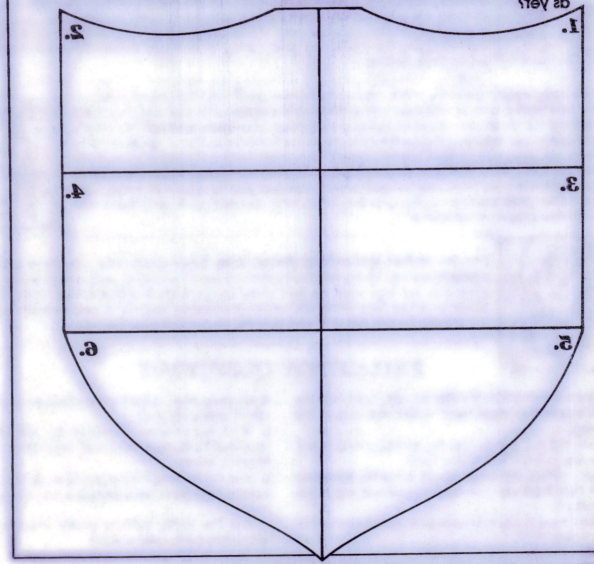

COAT OF ARMS

Make a coat of arms for yourself by drawing pictures of the following:

1. What occupies most of your time during the day?
2. What do you like to do when you are alone?
3. What do you like to do when you are with your family at home?
4. What do you like to do with your family when you are away from home?
5. What is your least favorite activity or chore?
6. What is something you have always wanted to do but have not done as yet?

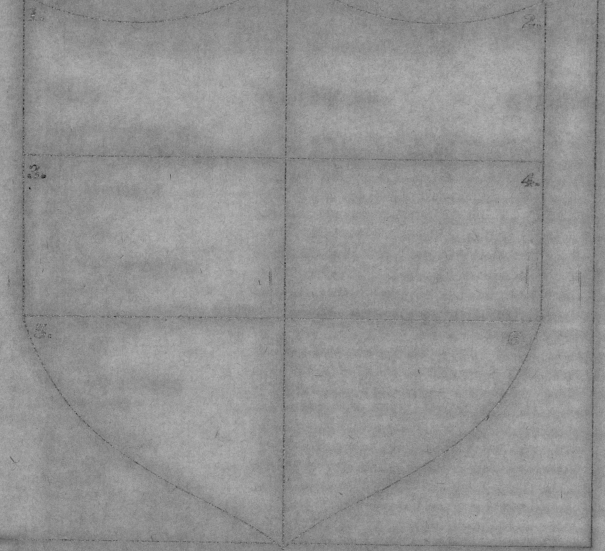

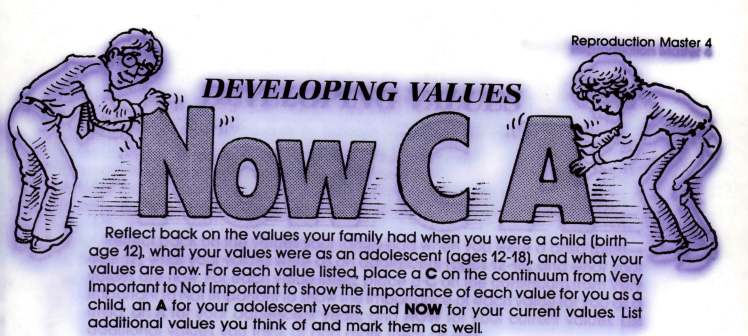

DEVELOPING VALUES
Now C A

Reflect back on the values your family had when you were a child (birth—age 12), what your values were as an adolescent (ages 12-18), and what your values are now. For each value listed, place a **C** on the continuum from Very Important to Not Important to show the importance of each value for you as a child, an **A** for your adolescent years, and **NOW** for your current values. List additional values you think of and mark them as well.

VALUES	VERY IMPORTANT	NOT IMPORTANT
Family Togetherness		
Extended Family		
Friends		
Neighborhood		
House		
Learning		
God		
Church Involvement		
Cleanliness		
Job		
Leisure Time		
Holidays		
Wealth		
Economic Security		
Self-Esteem		
Honesty		
The Law, Rules		
Freedom		
Feelings		
Resolving Conflicts		
Expression of Affection		
Expression of Anger		

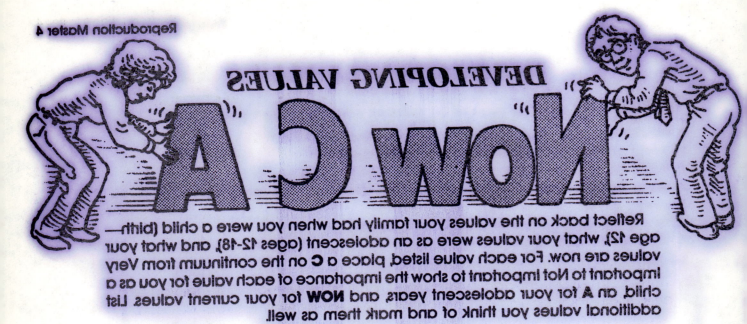

Family Togetherness		
Extended Family		
Friends		
Neighborhood		
House		
Learning		
God		
Church Involvement		
Cleanliness		
Job		
Leisure Time		
Holidays		
Wealth		
Economic Security		
Self-Esteem		
Honesty		
The Law, Rules		
Freedom		
Feelings		
Resolving Conflicts		
Expression of Affection		
Expression of Anger		

DISCOVERING VALUES
Now Ca...

VALUES	VERY IMPORTANT	NOT IMPORTANT
Family Togetherness		
Extended Family		
Friends		
Neighborhood		
Home		
Learning		
Cash		
Church Involvement		
Education		
Job		
Leisure Time		
Holidays		
Wealth		
Responsible Lifestyle		
Retirement		
Health		
The New State		
Freedom		
Destiny		

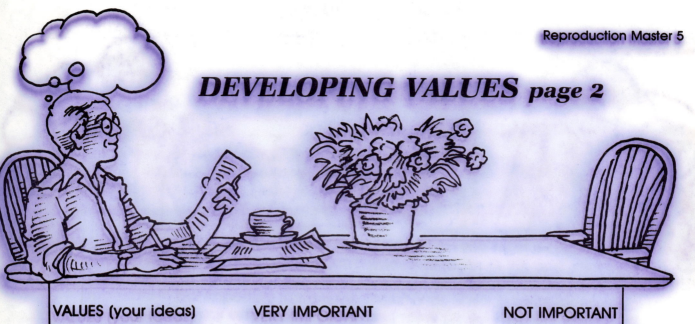

DEVELOPING VALUES *page 2*

VALUES (your ideas)	VERY IMPORTANT	NOT IMPORTANT

TIME FOR REFLECTION

I notice that . . .

I am surprised to see that . . .

I am not surprised to see that . . .

Two areas I would like to change are:

1.

2.

DEVELOPING VALUES page 2

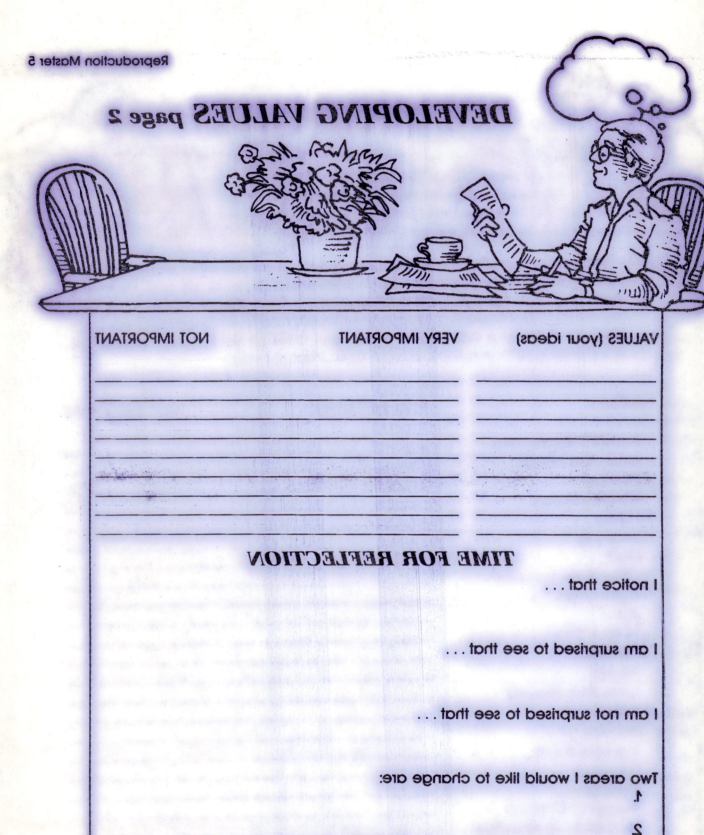

VALUES (your ideas)	VERY IMPORTANT	NOT IMPORTANT

TIME FOR REFLECTION

I notice that . . .

I am surprised to see that . . .

I am not surprised to see that . . .

Two areas I would like to change are:

1.

2.

DEVELOPING VALUES page 2

VALUES (your ideas)	VERY IMPORTANT	NOT IMPORTANT

TIME FOR REFLECTION

I notice that . . .

I am surprised to see that . . . .

I am not surprised to see that . . .

Two areas I would like to change are:
1
2

JESUS AND VALUES

SCRIPTURE REFERENCES	What We Learn from Jesus Through		Family Situations Where These Teachings Can Help
	His Teachings	His Example	
Matthew 4:1-11 (Temptation of Jesus)			
Luke 7:36-50 (Jesus' Feet Anointed)			
John 8:2-11 (Jesus and the Adulterous Woman)			
Luke 10:38-42 (Jesus with Mary and Martha)			
Mark 2:23-28 (Lord of the Sabbath)			
Luke 18:15-17 (Jesus with Children)			
Luke 19:1-10 (Jesus and Zaccheus)			
John 13:3-5, 12-17 (Jesus Washing the Disciples' Feet)			

JESUS AND VALUES

SCRIPTURE REFERENCES	What We Learn from Jesus Through		Family Situations Where These Teachings Can Help
	His Teachings	His Example	
Matthew 4:1-11 (Temptation of Jesus)			
Luke 7:36-50 (Jesus' Feet Anointed)			
John 8:2-11 (Jesus and the Adulterous Woman)			
Luke 10:38-42 (Jesus with Mary and Martha)			
Mark 2:23-28 (Lord of the Sabbath)			
Luke 18:15-17 (Jesus with Children)			
Luke 19:1-10 (Jesus and Zaccheus)			
John 13:3-5, 12-17 (Jesus Washing the Disciples' Feet)			

JESUS AND VALUES

SCRIPTURE REFERENCES	What We Learn from Jesus Through		Family Situations Where These Teachings Can Help
	His Teachings	His Example	
Matthew 4:1-11 (Temptation of Jesus)			
Luke 7:36-50 (Jesus Feet Anointed)			
John 8:2-11 (Jesus and the Adulterous Woman)			
Luke 10:38-42 (Jesus with Mary and Martha)			
Mark 2:23-28 (Lord of the Sabbath)			
Luke 18:15-17 (Jesus with Children)			
Luke 19:1-10 (Jesus and Zacchaeus)			
John 13:3-5, 12-17 (Jesus Washing the Disciples' Feet)			

CHRISTIAN VALUES

The Scriptures contain many guidelines for helping us make decisions and establish values. Read the following references, state the value described in each reference, and identify family situations where these values can be used.

Scripture References	Statement of value	Family situations where these values can be used
Exodus 20:2, 3		
Exodus 20:4-6		
Exodus 20:7		
Exodus 20:8-11		
Exodus 20:12		
Exodus 20:13		
Exodus 20:14		
Exodus 20:15		
Exodus 20:16		
Exodus 20:17		
Read Galatians 5:22, 23. List qualities Paul says should exemplify the Christian.	Behaviors which would exemplify each quality.	Family situations where these qualities could be particularly helpful.

CHRISTIAN VALUES

The Scriptures contain many guidelines for helping us make decisions and establish values. Read the following references, state the value described in each reference, and identify family situations where these values can be used.

Scripture References	Statement of value	Family situations where these values can be used
Exodus 20:2, 3		
Exodus 20:4-6		
Exodus 20:7		
Exodus 20:8-11		
Exodus 20:12		
Exodus 20:13		
Exodus 20:14		
Exodus 20:15		
Exodus 20:16		
Exodus 20:17		
Read Galatians 5:22, 23. List qualities Paul says should exemplify the Christian.	Behaviors which would exemplify each quality.	Family situations where these qualities could be particularly helpful.

CHRISTIAN VALUES

The scriptures contain many guidelines for helping us make decisions and establish values. Read the following references, state the value described in each reference, and identify family situations where these values can be used.

Scripture References	Statement of value	Family situations where these values can be used
Exodus 20:2, 3		
Exodus 20:4-6		
Exodus 20:7		
Exodus 20:8-11		
Exodus 20:12		
Exodus 20:13		
Exodus 20:14		
Exodus 20:15		
Exodus 20:16		
Exodus 20:17		
Read Galatians 5:22, 23. List qualities Paul says should exemplify the Christian.	Behaviors which would exemplify each quality.	Family situations where these qualities could be particularly helpful.

CHRISTIAN VALUES

CONFLICTING VALUES

Often we are confronted by situations in which two or more values are in conflict. Identify the conflicting values in each of the following situations.

SITUATION	CONFLICTING VALUES		
	Value A	vs.	Value B
1. You put an ailing, elderly parent in a convalescent home against his or her wishes.			
2. Your child wants a stereo. All his friends have one.			
3. Your teenage daughter has run away from home and is living with her boyfriend.			
4. Some friends want you to buy a cabin with them. You would need to get a loan from the bank and work overtime to pay for it.			
5. You leave a resistant, angry child at home on a Sunday morning while you go to church.			
6. Your spouse has been abusive on a number of occasions. You consider divorce proceedings.			
7. Your best friend has told you he is unhappy in his marriage and is having an affair with another friend of yours.			
8. You are offered a job promotion, but it will mean relocating to another area. Your family is unanimously against the move.			
Other situations you think of:			

CONFLICTING VALUES

Often we are confronted by situations in which two or more values are in conflict. Identify the conflicting values in each of the following situations.

SITUATION	CONFLICTING VALUES		
	Value A	vs.	Value B
1. You put an ailing, elderly parent in a convalescent home against his or her wishes.			
2. Your child wants a stereo. All his friends have one.			
3. Your teenage daughter has run away from home and is living with her boyfriend.			
4. Some friends want you to buy a cabin with them. You would need to get a loan from the bank and work overtime to pay for it.			
5. You leave a resistant, angry child at home on a Sunday morning while you go to church.			
6. Your spouse has been abusive on a number of occasions. You consider divorce proceedings.			
7. Your best friend has told you he is unhappy in his marriage and is having an affair with another friend of yours.			
8. You are offered a job promotion, but it will mean relocating to another area. Your family is unanimously against the move.			
Other situations you think of:			

CONFLICTING VALUES

Often we are confronted by situations in which two or more values are in conflict. Identify the conflicting values in each of the following situations.

SITUATION	CONFLICTING VALUES		
	Value A	vs.	Value B
1. You put an ailing, elderly parent in a convalescent home against his or her wishes.			
2. Your child wants a stereo. All his friends have one.			
3. Your teenage daughter has run away from home and is living with her boyfriend.			
4. Some friends want you to buy a cabin with them. You would need to get a loan from the bank and work overtime to pay for it.			
5. You learn that a friend's house was robbed on a Sunday morning while you go to church.			
6. Your spouse has been abusive on a number of occasions. You consider divorce proceedings.			
7. Your best friend has told you he is unhappy in his marriage and is having an affair with another friend of yours.			
8. You are offered a job promotion, but it will mean relocating to another area. Your family is unanimously against the move.			
Other situations you think of:			

RESPONSIBILITIES OF PARENTING

Read through the list of words used to describe the responsibilities of parenting.

Then put a number next to each word to show your feelings regarding the importance of each task, with number 1 being the most important, and number 10 the least important task.

_____ Provider
_____ Friend
_____ Leader
_____ Teacher
_____ Disciplinarian
_____ Giver of hugs and love
_____ Guide
_____ Example
_____ _____ (another word you think of)
_____ _____ (another word you think of)

RESPONSIBILITIES OF PARENTING

Read through the list of words used to describe the responsibilities of parenting.

Then put a number next to each word to show your feelings regarding the importance of each task, with number 1 being the most important, and number 10 the least important task.

_____ Provider
_____ Friend
_____ Leader
_____ Teacher
_____ Disciplinarian
_____ Giver of hugs and love
_____ Guide
_____ Example
_____ (another word you think of)
_____ (another word you think of)

RESPONSIBILITIES OF PARENTING

Read through the list of words used to describe the responsibilities of parenting.

Then put a number next to each word to show your feelings regarding the importance of each task, with number 1 being the most important, and number 10 the least important task.

_____ Provider

_____ Friend

_____ Leader

_____ Teacher

_____ Disciplinarian

_____ Giver of hugs and love

_____ Guide

_____ Example

_____ (another word you think of)

_____ (another word you think of)

COMMUNICATION IN THE FAMILY

Identify authoritarian, permissive, and democratic responses for each of the following situations.

Situations	Authoritarian	Permissive	Democratic
1. Setting the table.			
2. Picking up clothes.			
3. Deciding what clothes to wear.			
4. Playing in the street.			
5. Doing homework.			
6. Spilling milk at dinner.			
7. Staying out past dark.			
8. Deciding if the child should take piano lessons.			
9. Deciding rules regarding the use of a video game.			
10. Having a friend stay overnight.			

COMMUNICATION IN THE FAMILY

Identify authoritarian, permissive, and democratic responses for each of the following situations.

Situations	Authoritarian	Permissive	Democratic
1. Setting the table.			
2. Picking up clothes.			
3. Deciding what clothes to wear.			
4. Playing in the street.			
5. Doing homework			
6. Spilling milk at dinner.			
7. Staying out past dark			
8. Deciding if the child should take piano lessons.			
9. Deciding rules regarding the use of a video game.			
10. Having a friend stay overnight.			

COMMUNICATION IN THE FAMILY

Identify authoritarian, permissive, and democratic responses for each of the following situations.

Situations	Authoritarian	Permissive	Democratic
1. Setting the table.			
2. Picking up clothes.			
3. Deciding what clothes to wear.			
4. Playing in the street.			
5. Doing homework.			
6. Spilling milk at dinner.			
7. Staying out past dark.			
8. Deciding if the child should take piano lessons.			
9. Deciding rules regarding the use of a video game.			
10. Having a friend stay overnight.			

FAMILY ACTIVITIES THAT BUILD VALUES
INFORMAL FAMILY ACTIVITIES

Bicycling	Visiting parent's place of employment
Hiking	Family night at the YMCA
Picnicking	Fishing
Swimming	Boating
Going to the zoo	Shopping
Miniature golfing	Camping
Going out for dessert	Taking a bus ride
Going to the beach	Taking the train on a short trip
Library visit	Inviting another family over for dinner
Playing at the park	Outing with each child alone
Museum visit	Going to a sports event
Airport visit	Visiting a convalescent home
Going to animal farm	Visiting relatives

MORE STRUCTURED LEARNING

Family Values Book—Ask family members to each choose a value—something that is important to them and then to draw a picture of it (or a situation in which this value is important). Draw pictures of as many values as time permits. Talk about the pictures. Then staple the pictures together into a booklet with a cover announcing, "The (name) Family Values Book."

Family Discussion—As a family, think of a situation in which someone had to make a decision between right and wrong. You may want to check your local newspaper for ideas. Or ask the child for a situation which might have happened at school. Talk together about different ways a person could act in this situation and what each family member feels is the right decision.

Family Council—Consider the possibility of holding a regular (weekly or biweekly) family council meeting for discussing family concerns, chores, responsibilities, decisions, and anything else that needs to be discussed. Be sure to set aside a special time when all family members will be present. Develop an agenda together. Then go item by item through the agenda, encouraging everyone to express feelings and opinions about the matters being discussed.

Squirms—Family members use index cards or slips of paper for writing down "What if ...?" questions that involve a decision regarding right and wrong, or best and worst. Questions should be placed in a coffee can or shoe box. Then have family members take turns drawing out a question and responding.

FAMILY ACTIVITIES THAT BUILD VALUES
INFORMAL FAMILY ACTIVITIES

Bicycling	Visiting parent's place of employment
Hiking	Family night at the YMCA
Picnicking	Fishing
Swimming	Boating
Going to the zoo	Shopping
Miniature golfing	Camping
Going out for dessert	Taking a bus ride
Going to the beach	Taking the train on a short trip
Library visit	Inviting another family over for dinner
Playing at the park	Outing with each child alone
Museum visit	Going to a sports event
Airport visit	Visiting a convalescent home
Going to animal farm	Visiting relatives

MORE STRUCTURED LEARNING

Family Values Book—Ask family members to each choose a value—something that is important to them and then to draw a picture of it (or a situation in which this value is important). Draw pictures of as many values as time permits. Talk about the pictures. Then staple the pictures together into a booklet with a cover announcing, "The (name) Family Values Book."

Family Discussion—As a family, think of a situation in which someone had to make a decision between right and wrong. You may want to check your local newspaper for ideas or ask the child for a situation which might have happened at school. Talk together about different ways a person could act in this situation and what each family member feels is the right decision.

Family Council—Consider the possibility of holding a regular (weekly or biweek-ly) family council meeting for discuss-ing family concerns, chores, responsi-bilities, decisions, and anything else that needs to be discussed. Be sure to set aside a special time when all fami-ly members will be present. Develop an agenda together. Then go item by item through the agenda, encourag-ing everyone to express feelings and opinions about the matters being dis-cussed.

Squirms—Family members use index cards or slips of paper for writing down "What if . . .?" questions that involve a decision regarding right and wrong, or best and worst. Questions should be placed in a coffee can or shoe box. Then have family members take turns drawing out a question and respond-ing.

FAMILY ACTIVITIES THAT BUILD VALUES

INFORMAL FAMILY ACTIVITIES

Bicycling	Visiting parent's place of employment
Hiking	Family night at the YMCA
Picnicking	Fishing
Swimming	Boating
Going to the zoo	Shopping
Miniature golfing	Camping
Going out for dessert	Taking a bus ride
Going to the beach	Taking the train on a short trip
Library visit	Inviting another family over for dinner
Playing at the park	Outing with each child alone
Museum visit	Going to a sports event
Airport visit	Visiting a convalescent home
Going to animal farm	Visiting relatives

MORE STRUCTURED LEARNING

Family Values Book—Ask family members to each choose a value—something that is important to them and then to draw a picture of it (or a situation in which this value is important). Draw pictures of as many values as time permits. Talk about the pictures, then staple the pictures together into a booklet with a cover announcing "The _____ (name) Family Values Book."

Family Discussion—As a family, think of a situation in which someone had to make a decision between right and wrong. You may want to check your local newspaper for ideas. Or ask the child for a situation which might have happened at school. Talk together about different ways a person could act in this situation and what each family member feels is the right decision.

Family Council—Consider the possibility of holding a regular (weekly or biweekly) family council meeting for discussing family concerns, chores, responsibilities, decisions, and anything else that needs to be discussed. Be sure to set aside a special time when all family members will be present. Develop an agenda together, then go item by item through the agenda, encouraging everyone to express feelings and opinions about the matters being discussed.

Questions—Family members use index cards or slips of paper for writing down "What if ...?" questions that involve a decision regarding right and wrong, or best and worst. Questions should be placed in a coffee can or shoe box, then have family members take turns drawing out a question and responding.

GUIDELINES
FOR WORKING THROUGH DIFFERENCES

Name of Parent   Name of Child   Age

Briefly define the issue as you (the parent) see it.

Briefly define the issues as the child sees it.

What specific areas for compromising are there?
   Parent's Perspective:

   Child's Perspective:

List three alternatives you think would resolve the issue.
   •
   •
   •

List three alternatives that the child thinks would resolve the issue.
   •

   •

   •

Read each other's alternatives and identify which one (or ones) you could both accept.

Decide together which alternative you will try. At a later time (such as if the issue comes up again), evaluate what happened, and decide whether or not another alternative should be used.

GUIDELINES
FOR WORKING THROUGH DIFFERENCES

Name of Parent _____ Name of Child _____ Age _____

Briefly define the issue as you (the parent) see it.

Briefly define the issues as the child sees it.

What specific areas for compromising are there?
Parent's Perspective:

Child's Perspective:

List three alternatives you think would resolve the issue.

•

•

•

List three alternatives that the child thinks would resolve the issue.

•

•

•

Read each other's alternatives and identify which one (or ones) you could both accept.

Decide together which alternative you will try. At a later time (such as if the issue comes up again), evaluate what happened, and decide whether or not another alternative should be used.

GUIDELINES
FOR WORKING THROUGH DIFFERENCES

Name of Parent   Name of Child   Age

Briefly define the issue as you (the parent) see it.

Briefly define the issue as the child sees it.

What specific areas for compromise are there?
   Parent's Perspective:

   Child's Perspective:

List three alternatives you think would resolve the issue.

List three alternatives that the child thinks would resolve the issue.

Read each other's alternatives and identify which one (or ones) you could both accept.

Decide together which alternative you will try. At a later time (such as if the issue comes up again), evaluate what happened, and decide whether or not another alternative should be used.

CASE STUDIES

Situation A
(Preschool-age child)

Four-year-old Sally doesn't want to wear the new outfit her grandmother just sent her for her birthday. In fact, all she wants to wear to preschool every day is the same pair of blue jeans and T-shirt. Several mornings Sally and her mother have argued about Sally's clothes, and both Sally and her mother have been in tears by the time she leaves for school.

Situation B
(Elementary-age child)

Johnny hates practicing his piano lessons after school. He would rather be out playing with his friends. Yesterday he announced, "I don't even want to take piano lessons anymore. One year is enough!"

Situation C (Adolescent young person)

Jenny talks on the phone constantly. In fact, few others in the family get to use it. Some of her father's clients are complaining that they always get a busy signal when they call.

CASE STUDIES

Situation A
(Preschool-age child)

Four-year-old Sally doesn't want to wear the new outfit her grandmother just sent her for her birthday. In fact, all she wants to wear to preschool every day is the same pair of blue jeans and T-shirt. Several mornings Sally and her mother have argued about Sally's clothes, and both Sally and her mother have been in tears by the time she leaves for school.

Situation B
(Elementary-age child)

Johnny hates practicing his piano lessons after school. He would rather be out playing with his friends. Yesterday he announced, "I don't even want to take piano lessons anymore. One year is enough!"

Situation C (Adolescent / young person)

Jenny talks on the phone constantly. In fact, few others in the family get to use it. Some of her father's clients are complaining that they always get a busy signal when they call.

CASE STUDIES

Situation A (Preschool-age child)

Four-year-old Sally doesn't seem to wear the new outfit her grandmother just sent her for her birthday. In fact, all she wants to wear to preschool every day is the same pair of blue jeans and T-shirt. Several mornings Sally and her mother have argued about Sally's clothes, and both Sally and her mother have been in tears by the time she leaves for school.

Situation B (Elementary-age child)

Johnny hates practicing his piano lesson after school. He would rather be out playing with his friends. Yesterday he announced, "I don't even want to take piano lessons anymore. One year is enough!"

Situation C (Adolescent young person)

Jenny talks on the phone constantly. In fact, few others in the family get to use it. Some of her father's clients are complaining that they always get a busy signal when they call.

LOOKING BACK, LOOKING FORWARD

As you reflect on this learning experience, complete the following sentences:

I especially appreciated learning that ...

I was surprised to learn that ...

I need to ...

My child (children) need to ...

When it comes to values, I feel most concerned about . . .

Something I want to change is . . .

I would like to enhance my home environment by . . .

Regarding values, I am most afraid about . . .

Next year at this time, I would like to have improved my relationship with my child (children) by doing the following:

LOOKING BACK, LOOKING FORWARD

As you reflect on this learning experience, complete the following sentences:

I especially appreciated learning that ...

I was surprised to learn that ...

I need to ...

My child (children) need to ...

When it comes to values, I feel most concerned about ...

Something I want to change is ...

I would like to enhance my home environment by ...

Regarding values, I am most afraid about ...

Next year at this time, I would like to have improved my relationship with my child (children) by doing the following:

LOOKING BACK, LOOKING FORWARD

As you reflect on this learning experience, complete the
following sentences:

I especially appreciated learning that ...

I was surprised to learn that ...

I need to ...

My child (children) need to ...

When it comes to values, I feel most concerned about ...

Something I want to change is ...

I would like to enhance my home environment by ...

Regarding values, I am most afraid about ...

Next year at this time, I would like to have improved my relationship with
my child (children) by doing the following:

EVALUATION OF LEARNING EXPERIENCE

Read through the following list as it relates to the course you have just completed. Circle the number which most closely reflects your feelings about each item.

ITEMS	Outstanding	Good	Fair	Poor	No Response
1. Warmth and friendliness of instructor.	1	2	3	4	5
2. Provided practical help for cultivating within my children the values about which I'm concerned.	1	2	3	4	5
3. Variety of learning experiences (discussion, lecture, etc.).	1	2	3	4	5
4. Helpful for me personally.	1	2	3	4	5
5. Helpful for my family.	1	2	3	4	5
6. Adequacy of learning environment (size and arrangement of room, comfortable chairs, etc.).	1	2	3	4	5
7. Strengthened my interest and involvement in Bible study.	1	2	3	4	5
8. Enriched my experience of praying (alone and in small groups).	1	2	3	4	5
9. Helped me meet new people and begin development of relationships with them.	1	2	3	4	5
10. Helped me deepen relationships with people I already knew.	1	2	3	4	5

Any additional comments or suggestions:

EVALUATION OF LEARNING EXPERIENCE

Read through the following list as it relates to the course you have just completed. Circle the number which most closely reflects your feelings about each item.

ITEMS	Outstanding	Good	Fair	Poor	No Response
1. Warmth and friendliness of instructor.	1	2	3	4	5
2. Provided practical help for cultivating within my children the values about which I'm concerned.	1	2	3	4	5
3. Variety of learning experiences (discussion, lecture, etc.).	1	2	3	4	5
4. Helpful for me personally.	1	2	3	4	5
5. Helpful for my family.	1	2	3	4	5
6. Adequacy of learning environment (size and arrangement of room, comfortable chairs, etc.).	1	2	3	4	5
7. Strengthened my interest and involvement in Bible study.	1	2	3	4	5
8. Enriched my experience of praying (alone and in small groups).	1	2	3	4	5
9. Helped me meet new people and begin development of relationships with them.	1	2	3	4	5
10. Helped me deepen relationships with people I already knew.	1	2	3	4	5

Any additional comments or suggestions:

EVALUATION OF LEARNING EXPERIENCE

Read through the following list as it relates to the course you have just completed. Circle the number which most closely reflects your feelings about each item.

ITEMS	Outstanding	Good	Fair	Poor	No Response
1. Warmth and friendliness of instructor.	1	2	3	4	5
2. Provided practical help for cultivating within my children the values about which I'm concerned.	1	2	3	4	5
3. Variety of learning experiences (discussion, lecture, etc.).	1	2	3	4	5
4. Helpful for me personally.	1	2	3	4	5
5. Helpful for my family.	1	2	3	4	5
6. Adequacy of learning environment (size and arrangement of room, comfortable chairs, etc.).	1	2	3	4	5
7. Strengthened my interest and involvement in Bible study.	1	2	3	4	5
8. Enriched my experience of praying (alone and in small groups).	1	2	3	4	5
9. Helped me meet new people and begin development of relationships with them.	1	2	3	4	5
10. Helped me deepen relationships with people I already knew.	1	2	3	4	5

Any additional comments or suggestions:

CELEBRATION RESPONSIVE READING

LEADER: Let us reflect with gratitude upon what we have experienced in these sessions.

MEN: We are grateful for other people with whom we can learn and share,

WOMEN: People who can encourage us as we grow as parents and families,

LEFT: Those who can pray for us,

RIGHT: And for whom we can pray.

LEADER: We are grateful for God's Word,

WOMEN: A guide in facing moral decisions,

MEN: Whether they are difficult or simple;

LEFT: For the Holy Spirit, who helps us understand and act upon God's Word;

RIGHT: And for the ability to think—a marvelous, God-created gift.

LEADER: We are grateful for God's love,

MEN: For the promise that God is always with us

WOMEN: And is concerned about whatever we are experiencing.

LEFT: We are grateful for the courage God gives us to do what is right.

RIGHT: And for the strength to face challenges which seem impossible.

LEADER: We are grateful for our children,

WOMEN: Who enrich our lives

MEN: And help us grow,

LEFT: Who sometimes stretch us to the limit,

RIGHT: And at other times teach us important lessons.

LEADER: We are not alone. God is always with us, God's Spirit moves and teaches and motivates us.

LEFT: We are not alone. We have each other,

RIGHT: And we have our families.

EVERY-ONE: To God be the glory, for God is doing great things—in each one of us, and in our families.

CELEBRATION RESPONSIVE READING

LEADER: Let us reflect with gratitude upon what we have experienced in these sessions.

MEN: We are grateful for other people with whom we can learn and share,

WOMEN: People who encourage us as we grow as parents and families,

LEFT: Those who can pray for us.

RIGHT: And for whom we can pray.

LEADER: We are grateful for God's Word,

WOMEN: A guide in facing moral decisions,

MEN: Whether they are difficult or simple;

LEFT: For the Holy Spirit, who helps us understand and act upon God's Word;

RIGHT: And for the ability to think—a marvelous, God-created gift.

LEADER: We are grateful for God's love,

MEN: For the promise that God is always with us

WOMEN: And is concerned about whatever we are experiencing.

LEFT: We are grateful for the courage God gives us to do what is right.

RIGHT: And for the strength to face challenges which seem impossible.

LEADER: We are grateful for our children,

WOMEN: Who enrich our lives

MEN: And help us grow.

LEFT: Who sometimes stretch us to the limit,

RIGHT: And at other times teach us important lessons.

LEADER: We are not alone. God is always with us. God's Spirit moves and teaches and motivates us.

LEFT: We are not alone. We have each other.

RIGHT: And we have our families.

EVERYONE: To God be the glory, for God is doing great things—in each one of us and in our families.

CELEBRATION RESPONSIVE READING

LEADER: Let us reflect with gratitude upon what we have experienced in these sessions.

MEN: We are grateful for other people with whom we can learn and share,

WOMEN: People who can encourage us as we grow as parents and families,

LEFT: Those who can pray for us,

RIGHT: And for whom we can pray.

LEADER: We are grateful for God's Word,

WOMEN: A guide in facing moral decisions,

MEN: Whether they are difficult or simple;

LEFT: For the Holy Spirit, who helps us understand and act upon God's Word;

RIGHT: And for the ability to think—a marvelous, God-created gift.

LEADER: We are grateful for God's love,

MEN: For the promise that God is always with us

WOMEN: And is concerned about whatever we are experiencing.

LEFT: We are grateful for the courage God gives us to do what is right.

RIGHT: And for the strength to face challenges which seem impossible.

LEADER: We are grateful for our children,

WOMEN: Who enrich our lives

MEN: And help us grow,

LEFT: Who sometimes stretch us to the limit,

RIGHT: And at other times teach us important lessons.

LEADER: We are not alone. God is always with us, God's Spirit moves and teaches and motivates us.

LEFT: We are not alone. We have each other,

RIGHT: And we have our families.

EVERY-ONE: To God be the glory, for God is doing great things—in each one of us, and in our families.

CELEBRATION RESPONSIVE READING

LEADER: Let us reflect with gratitude upon what we have experienced in these sessions.

MEN: We are grateful for other people with whom we can learn and share,

WOMEN: People who encourage us as we grow as parents and families,

LEFT: Those who can pray for us.

RIGHT: And for whom we can pray.

LEADER: We are grateful for God's Word,

WOMEN: A guide in facing moral decisions,

MEN: Whether they are difficult or simple;

LEFT: For the Holy Spirit, who helps us understand and act upon God's Word;

RIGHT: And for the ability to think—a marvelous, God-created gift.

LEADER: We are grateful for God's love,

MEN: For the promise that God is always with us

WOMEN: And is concerned about whatever we are experiencing.

LEFT: We are grateful for the courage God gives us to do what is right.

RIGHT: And for the strength to face challenges which seem impossible.

LEADER: We are grateful for our children,

WOMEN: Who enrich our lives

MEN: And help us grow,

LEFT: Who sometimes stretch us to the limit;

RIGHT: And at other times teach us important lessons.

LEADER: We are not alone. God is always with us; God's Spirit moves and teaches and motivates us.

LEFT: We are not alone. We have each other,

RIGHT: And we have our families.

EVERY-ONE: To God be the glory, for God is doing great things—in each one of us, and in our families.

CELEBRATION RESPONSIVE READING

LEADER: Let us reflect with gratitude upon what we have experienced in these sessions.

MEN: We are grateful for other people with whom we can learn and share,

WOMEN: People who can encourage us as we grow as parents and families,

LEFT: Those who can pray for us

RIGHT: And for whom we can pray.

LEADER: We are grateful for God's Word,

WOMEN: A guide in facing moral decisions,

MEN: Whether they are difficult or difficult

LEFT: For the Holy Spirit, and not upon God's Word

RIGHT: And for the ability, this, God-created gift

LEADER: We are grateful

MEN: For the promise that God is always with us

WOMEN: And is concerned about what we are experiencing,

LEFT: We are grateful for the courage God gives us to do what is right

RIGHT: And for the strength to face challenges which seem impossible.

LEADER: We are grateful for our children,

WOMEN: Who enrich our lives

MEN: And help us grow,

LEFT: Who sometimes stretch us to the

RIGHT: And at other times teach us important lessons

LEADER: We are not alone. God is always with us. God's Spirit moves and teaches and motivates us.

LEFT: We are not alone. We have each other.

RIGHT: And we have our families.

EVERY-ONE: To God be the glory, for God is doing great things—in each one of us, and in our families.